CHURCH POTLUCK
CARRY-INS AND CASSEROLES

Homestyle recipes for church suppers, family gatherings, and community celebrations

SUSIE SIEGFRIED

ADAMS MEDIA
AVON, MASSACHUSETTS

Published by Adams Media, an F+W Publications Company
57 Littlefield Street
Avon, MA 02322
www.adamsmedia.com

ISBN: 1-59337-549-2

Printed in Canada.

J   I   H   G   F   E   D   C   B   A

Library of Congress Cataloging-in-Publication Data
Siegfried, Susie.
Church potluck carry-ins and casseroles : homestyle recipes for church suppers,
family gatherings, and community celebrations / Susie Siegfried.
p.   cm.
ISBN 1-59337-549-2
1. Cookery, American. 2. Church dinners. I. Title.
TX715.S578 2006
641.5973—dc22
2005033318

Many of the designations used by manufacturers and sellers to distinguish their products are claimed as
trademarks. Where those designations appear in this book and Adams Media was aware of a trademark
claim, the designations have been printed in initial capital letters.

This publication is designed to provide accurate and authoritative information with regard to the subject matter covered. It is sold with the understanding that the publisher is not engaged in rendering legal, accounting,
or other professional advice. If legal advice or other expert assistance is required, the services of a competent
professional person should be sought.

—From a *Declaration of Principles* jointly adopted by a Committee of the
American Bar Association and a Committee of Publishers and Associations

Unless otherwise noted, the Bible used as a source is *The Holy Bible: King James Version*.

This book is available at quantity discounts for bulk purchases.
For information, please call 1-800-872-5627.

To all of you who were so willing to share your time, your favorite recipes and your love of cooking

Acknowledgments

This book would not exist without the help of many others. I would like to extend my thanks and appreciation to all who have contributed in any way. Many friends pitched in and contributed to the many recipes featured. I am very grateful to you all for your fabulous recipes and willingness to share them with me. In a cookbook with over 300 recipes, it is impossible to thank you all in this context, but please know how grateful I am to you. In particular, I must thank Annis and Laura for a number of dishes. You two have been an invaluable source of delicious treats that I am glad to share with everyone. I would also like to thank my dear friends, especially Kathi, for many hours of help. Lauren and Paula were essential to me in the typing of the book. Without them, I would still be pecking away! Thank you to Adams Media (especially Paula Munier, Andrea Norville, Jason Flynn, Brett Palana-Shanahan, and Casey Ebert) and everyone involved in the production of the book for your help. It is greatly appreciated. Lastly, I would like to thank my family, whom I hold very dear. Thank you to my husband, my children, my sisters, my sister-in-law Gayle, my cousin Barbara, and my wonderful friends for their love and support. I hope everyone enjoys these wonderful recipes as much as I do. Thank you to you all. God bless.

Hugs,
Susie Siegfried

Contents

Give us this day our daily bread.

—*Matthew 6:11*

Introduction

There's something really special about potlucks and carry-ins—the excitement of getting together with friends and family, meeting new people, enjoying good conversation, and then there's the food. I've always gotten a thrill out of finding a fabulous new recipe at a potluck event. Not only do I love the anticipation of trying all the new and different dishes, I also love sharing some of my very favorite recipes with others and hope they will enjoy them as much as I do. Love of God, good food, and getting together with loved ones go hand in hand.

Do you know where the term *potluck* comes from? It came about partly by way of when uninvited guests would stop by, they would be offered whatever was left in the pot, so to speak. The food left over, the pot, and whether what was in the pot was good or bad, the luck! Hence, the term *potluck*!

I love going to potluck picnics and parties, whether it be at a friend or family member's home, a church social, office parties, you name it. Even when these events aren't held in or sponsored by a church, there's always a sense of tradition, community, and trust involved in them that reminds me of attending services.

That's why I'm always eager to participate whenever someone wants to hold a new potluck gathering. It makes me feel like I'm part of a new community tradition.

Why not take an opportunity to create your own potluck tradition? One of my favorites is every Christmas a group of us have a Christmas cookie party. Everyone brings all kinds of cookies. We all bring along the recipes as well, so we can exchange them with each other and share them with our family and friends during the holidays.

So many of my dear friends, new and old, were kind enough to share some of their favorite recipes with me for this book. I feel so blessed. I absolutely love being given recipes that are old family favorites or ones they have created themselves. Not everyone is willing to share his or her recipes, especially ones that have been handed down from generation to generation. So, it's particularly nice when others so generously share some of their very favorite recipes.

Many, many thanks to each one of you who have shared your recipes with me for this cookbook. Without your willingness to bestow some of your own unique recipes, this book could not have been possible. May God bless all of you, my dear family and friends, and all of you who are enjoying these recipes.

God bless and peace,

Susie Siegfried

Appetizers

*L*ast Thanksgiving I decided to prepare the big bird, a twenty-two-pound turkey, on the grill instead of roasting it in the oven. My sister-in-law, Gayle, had mentioned that a couple of her friends always put it on the grill and the result was moist and tender. It sounded like a great idea to me. Doing so would also make it easier to prepare the other dishes, since the oven would be available for all the other food we would be baking.

We looked up instructions online on grilling a turkey. We wrapped the turkey per instructions, started the grill—and how easy it was! We checked the turkey a time or two, then got busy fixing a ham, preparing our traditional oyster stuffing, making gravy, and greeting everyone as they began gathering for our holiday dinner.

Then my husband Larry walked into the kitchen and casually said, "You know the glass on the grill is cracked, don't you?" Gayle and I looked at each other and ran out to check the grill and our turkey. The glass wasn't just cracked—it had exploded! The glass was all over the deck and all over the foil as well. What a mess. We couldn't tell whether the glass had gotten into the turkey. We looked it over once and decided that the turkey and the grill both had to go. I was glad that I had a ham baking in the oven. Needless to say, we still had a wonderful time in spite of our turkey mishap.

I went out and bought a new grill to try it again next year, but this time my grill will be minus one item—the glass! It's given us a laugh or two now, but it wasn't so funny then and luckily none of us was out there when it happened. ～

Crispy Chicken Strips

These chicken strips are now a must for our family Christmas. We always have a lot of finger food at home to nibble during our Christmas party. The younger ones aren't so fond of some of these finger foods. But they love these chicken fingers and it seems like I can never make enough of them.

2 cups mashed potato flakes
½ teaspoon onion powder
2 cups seasoned bread crumbs
4 eggs, beaten
4 tablespoons milk
3 pounds chicken tenders
2 to 4 tablespoons vegetable oil
Honey mustard sauce or sweet and sour sauce

1. In a large bowl, combine potato flakes, onion powder, and bread crumbs.
2. In a smaller bowl, beat together eggs and milk.
3. Dip chicken into egg mixture, then into potato crumb mixture.
4. In a large skillet, over medium heat, cook chicken in oil, turning to avoid burning.
5. Cook 5 to 7 minutes until golden.
6. Serve with honey mustard sauce or sweet and sour sauce.

❧ Serves 12 to 15

Rumaki

My friend Vicki used to make these hors d'oeuvres for the catering business that I had for ten years. Everything Vicki made for my store was fantastic. You know the saying "I never met a food I didn't like"? I never met any of Vicki's cooking that I didn't like!

1 cup teriyaki sauce
½ teaspoon minced jarred garlic
2 tablespoons brown sugar
2 8-ounce cans whole water chestnuts
1 pound bacon

1. In medium bowl, mix together teriyaki sauce, garlic, and brown sugar.
2. Put water chestnuts in marinade and marinate in refrigerator for 2 to 4 hours.
3. Slice bacon strips in half.
4. Wrap 1 piece of bacon around each water chestnut and secure with toothpick.
5. Broil, turning frequently, until bacon is almost crisp, about 5 to 10 minutes.
6. Put on paper towel and drain.
7. Can be served warm or cold.

❧ Makes 48

Hummus

This is a favorite recipe of my daughter Joelle. I use it for more than just an appetizer. We always like to have it when we have gyros, which she and I dearly love.

2 15-ounce cans garbanzo beans, drained
6 tablespoons yogurt
¼ cup olive oil
2½ tablespoons toasted sesame seeds
3 garlic cloves, diced
2 tablespoons lemon juice
½ teaspoon onion powder
Salt and pepper to taste

1. Purée all ingredients in blender.
2. Add extra oil if not smooth.
3. Refrigerate for 4 hours.
4. Serve cold with pita bread.

 Serves 10

Pauline's Cheese Ball

When my sister Lois shared this cheese ball recipe that her dear friend Pauline had given her nearly 45 years ago, I asked her if she was sure of the amounts called for. I couldn't believe the number of jars of cheese. She said that she makes two cheese balls but that Pauline made just one and it was HUGE. But it was great for a big crowd.

2 8-ounce packages cream cheese, softened
4 5-ounce jars pimiento and cheese
2 5-ounce jars cheese with chives
1 4.25-ounce jar finely chopped black olives
2 tablespoons grated onion
2 cups finely chopped nuts
Assorted crackers

1. In large bowl, combine all cheeses with electric beater and beat until smooth.
2. Blend in olives and onion.
3. Form into 2 cheese balls.
4. Put chopped nuts in a pie plate.
5. Roll cheese balls in nuts.
6. Refrigerate for 24 hours.
7. Serve with an assortment of crackers.

Serves 40 to 50

Cranberries with Cream Cheese

This is such a festive-looking appetizer that I especially like to take it to holiday parties. I also make a batch of it and keep it in my fridge to share with any friends who may drop in. It's become a holiday tradition.

1 cup water

1¼ cups sugar

1 12-ounce package fresh or frozen cranberries

½ cup orange marmalade

1 11-ounce can mandarin oranges, drained

1 tablespoon lemon juice

1 8-ounce package cream cheese at room temperature

Assorted crackers

1. In saucepan over medium heat, bring water and sugar to a boil without stirring. Boil for 5 minutes.
2. Add cranberries. Cook until berries pop and sauce is thickened, about 10 minutes.
3. Remove from heat.
4. Add orange marmalade and mandarin oranges to cranberry mixture.
5. Stir in lemon juice.
6. Cool.
7. Spoon over cream cheese. Serve with crackers.

✣ Yields 3 cups

Shrimp Cocktail Appetizer

Not only is this a great appetizer, but it makes a tasty meal as well. It's also good with imitation crab flakes or real crabmeat. I usually bring two of these when I am going to a party, as one is never enough.

1 8-ounce package cream cheese, softened

½ cup mayonnaise

½ teaspoon garlic powder

1 teaspoon onion powder

¾ to 1 cup cocktail sauce

1 pound frozen cooked shrimp, thawed

2 or 3 tablespoons parsley

Assorted crackers

1. Blend cream cheese, mayonnaise, garlic powder, and onion powder in a small bowl, whisking until creamy.
2. Spread on serving plate, covering entire plate.
3. Spoon cocktail sauce over the mixture.
4. Rinse shrimp with cold water. Drain and pat dry with paper towels.
5. Place shrimp evenly over cocktail sauce.
6. Sprinkle with parsley.
7. Refrigerate until time to serve.
8. Serve with an assortment of crackers.

✣ Serves 20 to 24

Spicy Scoops

Here's another recipe from my dear friend Vicki. I've made the recipe a lot easier by using the new tortilla scoops that are now on our grocery shelves. These are very tasty, and you can make them spicier by using a medium to hot salsa.

1 16-ounce package spicy sausage

1 bag tortilla scoops

2 cups salsa

2 cups cubed American cheese

¼ cup scallions

Cherry tomatoes

1. Brown sausage in skillet and drain.
2. Preheat oven to 350°
3. Put one tortilla scoop in each muffin tin cup.
4. Mix together all remaining ingredients except tomatoes in bowl.
5. Spoon mixture into scoops until they are ⅔ full.
6. Bake for 5 minutes.
7. Remove and garnish with a cherry tomato.

 Makes 48

Beefy Cheese Dip

It's been a while since Lois has brought this to our family Christmas celebration. She rediscovered this recipe while she was collecting some of her favorites for me. We've all enjoyed it; I can hardly wait until Christmas, when she's promised to make it again.

1 2.75-ounce jar dried beef

½ cup sour cream

1 8-ounce package cream cheese, softened

¼ cup chopped onion

¼ cup chopped green peppers

¼ teaspoon garlic powder

Assorted crackers

1. Preheat oven to 350°.
2. Chop dried beef into small pieces.
3. Mix all ingredients together.
4. Place in greased 8" square baking dish and cook for 10 to 15 minutes or until warm.
5. Serve with crackers.

Serves 6 to 8

Now the feast of unleavened bread drew nigh, which is called the Passover.

—*Luke 22:1*

Lois's Cheese Ball

Another cheese ball. My sister Lois spoils my daughter by bringing this when she comes to visit. She knows that it is absolutely Stacey's favorite cheese ball. Stacey wants Aunt Lois to visit us more often!

1 8-ounce package cream cheese, softened
1 5-ounce jar Old English cheese
1 5-ounce jar Cheddar cheese
1 5-ounce jar pineapple cheese
1½ cups pecan pieces
Crackers or pita crisps

1. In large bowl, combine all cheeses and beat with electric mixer until smooth.
2. Form into ball.
3. Place pecans in pie plate and roll cheese ball in nuts until well covered.
4. Refrigerate until time to serve.
5. Serve with crackers or pita crisps.

🎀 Serves 25

Curry Chicken Spread

This delicious spread is generously shared with me, and now with you, by Amy and Hap. It's one of the terrific recipes they prepare for guests at their bed and breakfast inn in Stowe, Vermont. I know that those you prepare it for will enjoy every bite as much as their guests do.

2 cups shredded Monterey jack cheese
6 ounces cream cheese, softened
1 cup chopped green onions
⅔ cup Major Grey's chutney
1 tablespoon curry powder
1 teaspoon ginger
½ teaspoon salt
3 boneless skinless chicken breast halves, cooked and shredded
1 cup sour cream
½ teaspoon garlic powder
¼ teaspoon paprika
¼ teaspoon pepper
¼ to ½ cup raisins
½ cup toasted slivered or sliced almonds
Wheat crackers

1. Beat Monterey jack cheese, cream cheese, ¼ cup green onions, chutney, curry powder, ginger, and salt in a bowl until well mixed.

continued

(Curry Chicken Spread—continued)

2. Spread thinly onto a large serving platter. Cover and chill.
3. Mix chicken, sour cream, garlic powder, paprika, and pepper in a bowl.
4. Spread over cheese layer. Cover and chill for 4 to 24 hours.
5. Sprinkle the remaining ¾ cup chopped green onions around the edge of the cheese mixture when ready to serve.
6. Sprinkle the raisins and almonds over the center.
7. Serve with wheat crackers.

Makes 18 servings

And a basket of unleavened bread, cakes of fine flour mingled with oil, and wafers of unleavened bread anointed with oil, and their meat offering, and their drink offerings.

—*Numbers 6:15*

Mexican Cheesecake

This festive savory cheesecake will be great for any hungry crowd. It also was shared with me by Amy and Hap, who published it in their *Signature* cookbook highlighting some of their guests' favorite recipes. Now you and others can savor it, too.

1½ cups finely crushed tortilla chips
¼ cup melted butter
16 ounces cream cheese, softened
2 cups shredded Monterey jack cheese
2 cups sour cream
3 eggs
1 cup mild salsa
1 4-ounce can chopped green chilies
3 avocados
1 tomato, seeded and chopped
1 tablespoon lemon juice
1 teaspoon salt
1 teaspoon cumin
1 cup mild salsa, drained
Tortilla chips

1. Combine crushed tortilla chips and melted butter in a bowl. Stir to mix well. Press in the bottom of a lightly greased 9" springform pan. Bake at 350° for 10 minutes. Remove to cool on wire rack.

continued

(Mexican Cheesecake—continued)

2. Combine cream cheese and Monterey jack cheese in a large bowl. Beat with an electric mixer until light and fluffy. Beat in 1 cup sour cream. Add eggs and beat at a low speed until the ingredients are just combined. Stir in 1 cup salsa and the green chilies.
3. Pour mixture over tortilla crust in the pan. Bake at 350° for 50 to 60 minutes or until center is almost set. Remove to wire rack.
4. Spread 1 cup sour cream over the top. Let cool to room temperature.
5. Cover and chill for 3 to 24 hours.
6. Peel, pit, and mash the avocados in a bowl 1 hour before serving time. Add tomato, lemon juice, salt, and cumin. Stir with a fork until combined. Cover and chill.
7. Loosen the cheesecake from the side of the pan with a sharp knife, and remove the side. Set cheesecake on a serving platter.
8. Dollop avocado mixture alternately with the drained salsa around the edge of the cheesecake.
9. Serve with tortilla chips.

❧ Makes 20 servings

Pam's Party Ryes

If Pam doesn't bring these tasty, cheesy ryes to our Christmas party, we send her out to the grocery to get the ingredients for them. We *never* have our family Christmas without them. Keep them covered with foil until ready to serve at your next carry-in party.

1 pound ground beef
1 pound sausage
1 pound Velveeta cheese
2 loaves Party Rye Bread
1 teaspoon garlic powder
1 teaspoon onion powder
1 tablespoon Worcestershire sauce

1. Brown ground beef and sausage together in skillet over medium heat. Drain on paper towels to remove grease.
2. In saucepan, put drained meat mixture and add cheese; cook over medium heat until cheese melts.
3. Remove from heat and spread over rye bread.
4. Bake at 350° for 3 to 5 minutes or until golden brown.

❧ Makes 48 pieces

Hot Pepperoni Dip

Leah and her husband Franny have been friends of my sister Anita for many, many years, so I was so thrilled to have one of Leah's recipes for this book. I liked this one so much that I made two batches—one for the office picnic and one for everyone to enjoy at home.

1 8-ounce package cream cheese, softened
½ cup sour cream
1 teaspoon oregano
¼ teaspoon garlic powder
½ cup pizza sauce
¼ cup chopped green pepper
¼ cup chopped green onion
½ cup finely diced pepperoni
1 cup shredded mozzarella cheese
Crackers

1. Mix together cream cheese, sour cream, oregano, and garlic powder and spread on bottom of 10" pie plate.
2. Spread pizza sauce on top of cream cheese mixture.
3. Top with green pepper, onions, and pepperoni.
4. Bake at 350° for 10 to 13 minutes.
5. Remove from oven and sprinkle with mozzarella cheese and bake 5 minutes longer.
6. Serve with Wheat Thins or other crackers.

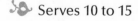 Serves 10 to 15

Florentine Cups

If you are short of time, you could purchase mini filo cups in the frozen food section of your grocery store. This is another of Vicki's recipes that has become a favorite.

3 eggs, slightly beaten
⅔ cup flour
½ teaspoon salt
1 cup milk
1½ cups sharp Cheddar cheese
3 tablespoons flour
3 eggs, slightly beaten
⅔ cup mayonnaise
1 10-ounce package frozen chopped spinach, thawed and drained
1 4-ounce can mushrooms, drained
6 bacon slices, fried, crisped, and crumbled

1. Combine eggs, ⅔ cups flour, salt, and milk and beat until smooth. Let stand 30 minutes.
2. Pour 2 tablespoons batter onto hot, lightly greased 8" griddle. Cook on one side only until underside is lightly browned. Place each mini crepe into a greased mini muffin tin cup.
3. In medium bowl, toss cheese with flour.
4. Add remaining ingredients, saving bacon for garnish and mix well. Fill cups with mixture.
5. Bake at 350° for 25 to 40 minutes or until set.
6. Top with bacon pieces.

Makes 12 cups

Sweet and Sour Chicken Bites

You can freeze these after cooking them—just reheat them at 350° for about 10 minutes.

1 egg
¼ cup flour
¼ cup cornstarch
¼ cup chicken broth
2 pounds chicken breasts, cubed
Vegetable oil for deep-frying

Sweet and Sour Sauce:
1 cup cider vinegar
1 cup chicken broth
1 cup brown sugar
2 tablespoons cornstarch
4 tablespoons water

1. Beat egg with a fork. Using fork, blend in flour, cornstarch, and chicken broth.
2. Put chicken into cornstarch batter, stirring to coat.
3. Put oil in deep fryer.
4. Deep-fry in small batches until golden brown.
5. Drain on paper towels.
6. In saucepan, combine vinegar, broth, and brown sugar. Bring to a boil on low to medium heat.
7. In small cup, mix cornstarch with cold water.
8. Slowly pour into boiling vinegar mixture while stirring. Stir over medium heat until thickened.
9. Pour over chicken when time to serve.

Serves 10 to 12

Cheese and Bacon Roll-Ups

My niece Janene and her husband Ron gave me this wonderfully tasty and super-easy recipe especially for this cookbook. They share a love of good food as well as a love of cooking with each other. They put lots of love into everything they make.

1 24-ounce loaf of Earth Grains Honey Wheatberry Bread, sliced and partially frozen
1 12-ounce tub of cream cheese with chives
1 pound bacon

1. Cut crust off bread.
2. Spread cream cheese on slices of bread.
3. Cut each slice of bread in half.
4. Cut raw bacon in thirds.
5. Roll up bread with cream cheese and wrap with bacon and secure with toothpick.
6. Bake on cookie sheet at 350° for 35 to 40 minutes.
7. Remove from cookie sheet and lay on paper towel to absorb.
8. Serve warm or cold.

Makes 25 roll-ups

Bob's Won Tons

My good friend Vicki's husband Bob makes the world's best won tons. I never order them in a Chinese restaurant because they don't have enough filling. Bob fills his with a generous amount of meat, and we happily stuff ourselves with these outrageously delicious appetizers.

1 pound ground pork

¼ teaspoon salt

1 tablespoon vegetable oil

1 tablespoon white wine

1 egg

1 teaspoon Accent

2 beaten eggs

1 package won ton wrappers

Vegetable oil for deep-frying

Sauce:

½ cup water

2 tablespoons cornstarch

6 tablespoons sugar

2 tablespoons soy sauce

1 tablespoon white wine

3 tablespoons white vinegar

½ cup pineapple juice

3 tablespoons ketchup

1. Mix together pork, salt, oil, wine, 1 egg, and Accent.
2. Put a spoonful of mixture on won ton wrapper and bring opposite corners together forming a triangle. Overlap corners and seal edges with beaten egg.
3. Line a 9" × 13" baking dish with waxed paper and layer won tons.
4. Cover top layer with foil.
5. Cook immediately or freeze overnight.
6. Cook in hot oil at 375° until golden brown.
7. Drain and serve.
8. In cup, mix together water and cornstarch.
9. In saucepan, mix sugar, soy sauce, wine, vinegar, pineapple juice, and ketchup.
10. Bring to a boil and add cornstarch mixture, stirring until it thickens.
11. When thick, remove from heat and cool.

Serves 48

Breakfast, Breads, and Brunch

Breaking Bread

All of us have many stories about our cooking experiences. Most of them we can look back and recall with laughter and fond memories; other stories are still bittersweet, and some we don't want to recall at all.

I remember back when I was engaged and was going to dinner at my future in-laws' house for the third time or so. Larry's mother, Gladys, was busy cooking in the kitchen. Wanting to make a good impression, I asked if I could be of any help. She had me help set the table and fix the drinks, but then she asked me to put a brown paper bag over her loaf of bread baking in the oven to help prevent it from burning.

Well, she had a gas stove. You can probably guess the rest. I removed the bread from the oven, placed it in the sack, and started to put it back in the oven. Somehow—to this day, I don't know how—I managed to catch the bag on fire. It must have been too close to one of the burners. She was in the other room and, of course, she walked in while I was attempting to put out the fire. I got so nervous, I took the whole bag and put it in the sink and sprayed it all with water. Her homemade bread was ruined, and I was the one who ruined it! What a way to start out with your soon-to-be mother-in-law. I appreciated her graciousness in taking it so well and making me feel welcomed to the family. Now that I am a new mother-in-law with a very sweet daughter-in-law, I will do my best to make her feel just as welcome in our family.

Favorite Coffeecake

My sister Marilyn has two coffeecake recipes that I'm including in this book. This one is my favorite, but I'm outnumbered by my other sisters—the other is their favorite. But believe me, I'll willingly eat either one.

½ cup shortening

¾ cup sugar

1 teaspoon vanilla

3 eggs

2 cups flour

1 teaspoon baking powder

1 teaspoon baking soda

1 cup sour cream

6 tablespoons butter

1 cup packed brown sugar

2 teaspoons cinnamon

1 cup chopped pecans

1. Cream shortening, sugar, and vanilla.
2. Add eggs one at a time, beating well.
3. Mix dry ingredients and add alternately with sour cream.
4. Spread half the batter in greased and floured tube pan.
5. Cream butter, brown sugar, and cinnamon. Add nuts and sprinkle over batter. Add remaining batter.
6. Bake at 350° on low rack in oven for 50 to 60 minutes.

Serves 14 to 16

My Sisters' Favorite Coffeecake

Here is my three sisters' favorite coffeecake recipe. Whenever we have a get-together at Marilyn's house, Marilyn has this ready for us when we walk in the door.

2 sticks margarine, softened

2 cups sugar

1 teaspoon vanilla

2 eggs

2 cups flour

1 teaspoon baking soda

¼ teaspoon salt

1 cup sour cream

¼ cup brown sugar

½ teaspoon cinnamon

1 cup pecan pieces

1. Cream margarine, sugar, and vanilla.
2. Add eggs one at a time, beating well.
3. Mix together flour, baking soda, and salt.
4. Add half of flour mixture, then half of sour cream; repeat until all of sour cream and flour mixture are combined.
5. In a greased and floured bundt pan, spread half of batter.
6. Mix together brown sugar, cinnamon, and pecans.
7. Sprinkle mixture over batter.
8. Add remaining batter.
9. Bake at 350° for 40 to 50 minutes.

Serves 14 to 16

Blueberry French Toast

I love blueberries—and they're a good healthy food, too. This recipe has been a favorite of mine for a while. It's also delicious when made with peaches or raspberries in place of the blueberries. Put the sauce in a container that you can use when serving.

12 slices day-old white bread

2 8-ounce packages cream cheese

1 cup fresh or frozen blueberries

12 eggs

2 cups milk

1/3 cup honey

Sauce:

1 cup sugar

2 tablespoons cornstarch

1 cup water

1 cup blueberries

1 tablespoon butter

1. Cut bread into 1" cubes and place half in a greased 9" × 13" baking dish.
2. Cut cream cheese into 1" cubes and place over bread.
3. Top with blueberries and remaining bread.
4. In a large bowl, beat eggs and add milk and honey, mixing well.
5. Pour over blueberries.
6. Cover and chill overnight.
7. Remove from refrigerator 30 minutes before baking.
8. Bake, covered with foil, at 350° for 30 minutes.
9. Uncover and bake 25 to 30 minutes more until golden brown and center is set.
10. In saucepan, combine sugar and cornstarch.
11. Add water and bring to a boil over medium heat.
12. Boil for 3 minutes, stirring constantly.
13. Stir in blueberries and reduce heat.
14. Simmer for 8 to 10 minute, stirring with whisk.
15. Stir in butter until melted.
16. Serve over French toast.

Serves 6 to 8

The LORD is my shepherd;
I shall not want.

—Psalms 23:1

Scrambled Eggs and Potatoes

Good for breakfast, brunch, even supper. Take this along to your next breakfast get-together. You can also use chicken and Mexican shredded cheese for a spicier flavor.

Butter cooking spray

1 32-ounce bag of frozen hash brown potatoes, thawed

1 cup chopped onion

½ cup chopped green pepper

½ cup chopped yellow pepper

1 16-ounce package bacon, fried crisp

12 eggs

¾ cup milk

Vegetable cooking spray

8 ounces shredded Cheddar cheese

1. Spray skillet with butter cooking spray and sauté potatoes until golden brown.
2. Add onions and peppers and cook a few minutes longer.
3. Break bacon into pieces and put on top of potatoes.
4. Remove from heat.
5. Mix together eggs and milk.
6. Spray skillet with vegetable cooking spray and scramble eggs until almost set.
7. Place potato mixture in greased 9" × 13" baking dish.
8. Sprinkle half the cheese over potatoes.
9. Put scrambled eggs on cheese and sprinkle remaining cheese over eggs.
10. Bake at 350° until cheese melts.

✎ Serves 8 to 10

Thou preparest a table before me in the presence of mine enemies: thou anointest my head with oil; my cup runneth over.

—Psalms 23:5

Raspberry Cream Cheese Coffeecake

Is there anything more delicious than the blending of raspberry and cream cheese? This luscious dish will definitely make your mouth water. Amy and Hap have outdone themselves with this appealing recipe.

2¼ cups flour

¾ cup sugar

¾ cup chilled unsalted butter, cut into pieces

½ teaspoon baking powder

½ teaspoon baking soda

¼ teaspoon salt

¾ cup sour cream

1 egg

1 teaspoon almond extract

1 8-ounce package cream cheese, softened

¼ cup sugar

1 egg

½ cup raspberry preserves

½ cup sliced almonds

1. In a large bowl, mix together flour and ¾ cup sugar.
2. Cut in the butter with a pastry blender until crumbly.
3. Remove 1 cup of mixture and set aside for topping.
4. Add the baking powder, baking soda, salt, sour cream, 1 egg, and almond extract to the remaining mixture.
5. Stir to mix well.
6. Spread evenly into the bottom and halfway up the sides of a greased 10" springform pan, using floured hands.
7. Combine the cream cheese, ¼ cup sugar, and 1 egg in a bowl.
8. Beat with an electric mixer until smooth.
9. Spread over the crust in the pan.
10. Top with the raspberry preserves.
11. Add the almonds to the reserved crumb mixture and sprinkle over the preserves.
12. Bake at 350° for 45 to 55 minutes or until the center is set and the crust is golden brown.
13. Remove to a wire rack and let cool completely.
14. Loosen from the sides of the pan with a sharp knife and remove from pan.
15. Refrigerate until ready to serve.

Serves 12

...on Crunch Muffins

These muffins fill your home with such a good smell that you'll have a hard time waiting for them to come out of the oven. You'll have to make an extra batch or you won't have enough to take with you. Another good one from Amy and Hap.

3 cups flour

1½ cups packed brown sugar

½ teaspoon salt

1 teaspoon cinnamon

1 teaspoon ginger

⅔ cup shortening

½ cup chopped walnuts or pecans

1 teaspoon cinnamon

2 teaspoons baking powder

½ teaspoon baking soda

2 eggs, beaten

1 cup buttermilk

1. In a large bowl, mix together flour, brown sugar, salt, 1 teaspoon cinnamon, and ginger.
2. Add the shortening and mix with fork until crumbly.
3. Remove ⅔ cup of the mixture to a small bowl.
4. Add the walnuts and 1 teaspoon cinnamon to the small bowl.
5. Stir to mix and set aside for topping.
6. Add the baking powder and baking soda to the shortening mixture in the large bowl and stir until just blended.
7. Add the eggs and buttermilk and stir until just combined.
8. Fill greased muffin cups ⅔ full.
9. Sprinkle the reserved topping evenly over the muffins.
10. Bake at 375° for 17 to 22 minutes or until a wooden toothpick inserted in the center comes out clean.
11. Cool in the pans for 3 to 5 minutes.
12. Remove to a wire rack to cool completely.

Makes 16

And unleavened bread, and cakes unleavened tempered with oil, and wafers unleavened anointed with oil: of wheaten flour shalt thou make them.

—Exodus 29:2

Apple French Toast

What's more American than apple pie? This apple French toast will please a group of hungry breakfasters even more than apple pie. Serve with cinnamon sugar for a wonderful treat.

1 stick butter

1 cup packed brown sugar

2 tablespoons light Karo syrup

4 large apples, peeled and thinly sliced

3 eggs

1 cup milk

1 tablespoon vanilla

8 slices (¾" thick) French bread

1. In a saucepan, melt butter.
2. Add brown sugar and syrup.
3. Cook over medium heat until bubbly.
4. Pour mixture into a greased 9" × 13" baking pan.
5. Layer apples on top.
6. In a bowl, beat eggs and add milk and vanilla and mix well.
7. Dip bread into egg mixture and layer over top of apples.
8. Cover and put in refrigerator overnight.
9. Bake uncovered at 350° for 35 minutes.
10. To serve, invert each slice of bread onto a serving plate and spoon apples over the top.

Serves 8 to 10

French Breakfast Puffs

Didn't you just love the smell of cinnamon wafting through the house when your mother baked? I occasionally put cinnamon sticks in water on top of my stove and simmer all day long—it brings back wonderful childhood memories, as do these puffs from my friend Annis.

⅓ cup shortening

½ cup sugar

1 egg

1½ cups flour

1½ teaspoons baking powder

¼ teaspoon nutmeg

½ teaspoon salt

½ cup milk

½ cup sugar

1 teaspoon cinnamon

½ cup melted butter

1. Preheat oven to 350°.
2. Grease muffin tins.
3. Mix together shortening, sugar, and egg.
4. Stir in flour, baking powder, nutmeg, and salt.
5. Alternating this mixture with milk, fill tins.
6. Bake 20 to 25 minutes.
7. Mix ½ cup sugar and cinnamon.
8. When puffs are done, dip in melted butter, then in cinnamon sugar mixture.

Makes 6

Annis's Coffeecake

Annis, my neighbor's mother, has been so wonderful to share many of her recipes for this book. She told me that this is best served warm and is great to take to a neighborhood morning gathering. It's also good if you have a church meeting or morning Bible study.

Vegetable cooking spray
2 8-ounce tubes of crescent rolls
1 8-ounce package of cream cheese
1¼ cups sugar
1 teaspoon vanilla
½ stick butter
1 teaspoon cinnamon

1. Spray a 9" × 13" baking pan with vegetable cooking spray.
2. Flatten 1 package of crescent rolls and place in bottom of pan.
3. Combine cream cheese, 1 cup sugar, and vanilla.
4. Spread over the first layer of crust.
5. Flatten the second package of crescent rolls and spread on top of this.
6. Melt butter and pour over the top of crust.
7. Mix together ¼ cup sugar and 1 teaspoon cinnamon.
8. Sprinkle over the top.
9. Bake for 30 minutes at 350° or until golden brown.
10. Serve with coffee.

Serves 8 to 10

Apple-Pumpkin Muffins

Do you know the muffin lady? I think it might be Annis, as she had so many muffin recipes to share with me. When the leaves are turning, it's time to make these—pumpkin just seems to go with autumn and the winter months ahead.

2½ cups flour
1 cup sugar
1 teaspoon cinnamon
1 teaspoon nutmeg
½ teaspoon allspice
½ teaspoon salt
1 cup pumpkin
½ cup vegetable oil
2 eggs, beaten
1 teaspoon vanilla
½ cup chopped pecans
1¾ cups peeled and finely chopped apples
½ cup packed dark brown sugar
2 teaspoons cinnamon
½ cup finely chopped pecans
2 tablespoons melted butter

1. In a bowl, combine flour, sugar, spices, and salt.
2. In another bowl, combine pumpkin, oil, eggs, vanilla, and ½ cup pecans and mix well.

continued

3. Add pumpkin mixture to dry ingredients and stir until moistened.
4. Fold in apples.
5. Spoon into greased muffin tins.
6. To make a streusel topping, combine dark brown sugar, 2 teaspoons cinnamon, ½ cup pecans, and melted butter.
7. Sprinkle topping over each muffin cup.
8. Bake at 350° for 35 to 40 minutes or until toothpick comes out clean.

✄ Makes 18

Feed the flock of God which is among you,
taking the oversight thereof, not by
constraint, but willingly; not for
filthy lucre, but of a ready mind.

—1 Peter 5:12

Banana-Oatmeal Muffins

Here's a great way to enjoy those bananas that you otherwise throw away. Surprise someone who needs a lift by taking these muffins to them and giving them a few minutes of your time. You can make someone's day a good one! These are from Annis.

1 cup flour
1¼ cups oats
3 teaspoons baking powder
½ teaspoon salt
¼ teaspoon cinnamon
⅓ cup oil
½ cup sugar
½ cup packed brown sugar
2 eggs
2 bananas mashed

1. In a bowl, combine flour, oats, baking powder, salt, and cinnamon, mixing well.
2. In another bowl, combine oil, sugars, eggs, and bananas, mixing well.
3. Combine mixtures and pour into greased muffin tins.
4. Bake at 400° for 20 minutes.

✄ Makes 1 dozen

Bran Muffins

These muffins that Annis shared with me are as moist as can be. This healthy combo of fruits and fiber never tasted so good. Just don't let the children know how good they are for you.

½ cup oats

1 cup All-Bran cereal

1 20-ounce can crushed pineapple, drained, with ½ cup plus 1 tablespoon juice reserved

1 egg, beaten

¾ cup sugar

1 teaspoon salt

¼ cup oil

1 cup buttermilk

1½ teaspoons baking soda

1½ cups flour

1 cup chopped walnuts

½ cup powdered sugar

1. In a bowl, combine oats and cereal.
2. In a small saucepan, place ½ cup of reserved pineapple juice and bring to boil.
3. Pour over cereal mixture and allow to cool.
4. Stir in egg and, mixing well, add remaining ingredients except 1 tablespoon pineapple juice and the powdered sugar.
5. Grease muffin tins and fill ¾ full of batter.
6. Bake at 400° for 15 minutes.
7. Cool slightly and remove from muffin pans.
8. In a small bowl, combine 1 tablespoon pineapple juice with the powdered sugar.
9. Stir until smooth.
10. Spoon glaze over baked muffins.
11. Orange juice can be used if you don't have enough pineapple juice.

Makes 18 to 20

Take heed therefore unto yourselves, and to all the flock, over the which the Holy Ghost hath made you overseers, to feed the church of God, which he hath purchased with his own blood.

—Acts 20:28

Ham and Egg Soufflé

This recipe has been used many times at our house. We even have it on Christmas morning so we can just pop it into the oven after making it the day before.

2½ cups cubed bread

1 pound deli ham, chipped

6 eggs

¼ teaspoon Worcestershire sauce

¾ teaspoon salt

¾ teaspoon pepper

¾ teaspoon dry mustard

⅛ teaspoon onion salt

1 cup half-and-half

1 cup milk

1½ cups shredded American and Cheddar cheeses

1. Spread bread and ham in bottom of greased 9" × 13" baking dish.
2. Blend together eggs, Worcestershire sauce, salt, pepper, dry mustard, onion salt, half-and-half, and milk in blender.
3. Pour over bread and meat.
4. Sprinkle shredded cheese over top of mixture. Cover and refrigerate overnight.
5. Remove from refrigerator 30 minutes before baking.
6. Bake at 325° for 40 to 45 minutes.

✦ Serves 8 to 10

Sweet Potato Biscuits

If you like sweet potatoes, you'll like these. This is a down-home recipe from Tennessee given to Annis by her cousin Janiv. These would also be very good served with honey butter.

1 cup mashed sweet potatoes

1 cup milk

½ cup sugar

1 beaten egg

1 tablespoon butter, melted

3 cups self-rising flour

1 teaspoon baking powder

½ cup vegetable shortening

Butter

Cinnamon sugar

1. In a medium bowl, mix sweet potatoes, milk, sugar, egg, and butter until well blended.
2. In a large bowl, combine flour and baking powder.
3. Use fork or pastry cutter to cut shortening into the flour-baking powder mixture.
4. Pour the sweet potato mixture into the flour mixture and mix well.
5. Drop potato mixture by large spoonfuls onto greased baking sheet.
6. Bake at 400° for 15 to 17 minutes or until golden.
7. Serve with butter and cinnamon sugar.

✦ Makes 18 to 20

Carrot Zucchini Bread

Can you imagine that this tasty, moist bread is healthy for you as well? It is a great combination of fruits and vegetables all rolled into one. Wrap it up, tie it with a bow, and surprise a friend with it.

1 cup unsweetened applesauce
¾ cup shredded carrots
¾ cup peeled and shredded zucchini
½ cup sugar
½ cup egg substitute
1½ teaspoons pumpkin pie spice
1 teaspoon ground cinnamon
½ teaspoon ground nutmeg
3 cups self-rising flour
¾ cup orange juice

1. In a bowl, combine the first 8 ingredients.
2. Add flour alternately with orange juice to carrot mixture.
3. Pour into 2 greased and floured 8" × 4" × 2" loaf pans.
4. Bake at 350° for 45 minutes or until bread tests indicate doneness.
5. Cool for 10 minutes; remove from pans to a wire rack to cool.

❧ Makes 2 loaves

Cherry Nut Bread

This is a super-easy bread recipe – no yeast required! This would be great with a topping of 2 tablespoons of sugar, ¼ teaspoon of cinnamon, and ½ cup slivered almonds. Be sure to add it before baking.

2 eggs
2 cups sugar
1 teaspoon salt
2 teaspoons baking soda
1 teaspoon almond extract
½ cup oil
2 cups flour
1 20-ounce can cherry pie filling
1 cup chopped nuts

1. Mix all ingredients together.
2. Pour into 2 greased and floured 9" × 5" × 3" loaf pans.
3. Bake at 350° for 1 hour.

❧ Makes 2 loaves

Cheesy Onion Bread

This is a good accompaniment for many meals. Take some lasagna and a salad along with this, and you'll have a complete meal for any family.

Vegetable cooking spray
1 tube frozen white bread, partially thawed
¼ cup melted butter or margarine
1 cup thinly sliced Vidalia onions
1 cup shredded asiago blend cheese

1. Spray 9" × 13" baking dish with vegetable cooking spray.
2. Cut unbaked bread into 20 slices. Place 10 of the slices in pan.
3. Drizzle butter onto slices of bread.
4. Place half of the sliced onions on the bread and top with half of the grated cheese.
5. Repeat layers.
6. Let rise 1 hour in warm place before baking.
7. Bake at 375° for 25 minutes.

Serves 10 to 14

Liz's Spoonbread

Here's another good southern recipe that I was introduced to by another Navy wife. Her husband was the commanding officer of the ship my husband was stationed on while we were in Virginia. I remember her for her gracious hospitality and this wonderful spoonbread.

4 eggs
4 cups milk
1 cup white cornmeal
1 tablespoon butter
½ teaspoon salt

1. Beat eggs with 1 cup of the milk.
2. Combine cornmeal, butter, salt, and the remaining 3 cups of milk.
3. Bring cornmeal mixture to a boil and stir.
4. Slowly blend egg and milk mixture into meal mixture.
5. Pour into a greased 2-quart casserole.
6. Place casserole in a pan of hot water.
7. Bake at 400° for 45 minutes.
8. Serve with butter.

Serves 9

Poppy Seed Bread

This recipe used to call for coconut pudding, but I can't find it anywhere in the grocery stores, so now I use vanilla pudding and add coconut flavoring. It's a good substitute for this delicious bread.

1 18.25-ounce package white cake mix

4 eggs

¼ cup poppy seed

½ cup cooking oil

1 cup hot water

1 3-ounce package vanilla instant pudding

1 teaspoon coconut flavoring

1. In large bowl, combine all ingredients and beat for 4 minutes.
2. Bake at 350° for 30 to 40 minutes in 2 waxed-paper-lined 9" × 5" × 2" pans.

❧ Makes 2 loaves

My Mom's Nut Bread

This is the only recorded recipe we have of my mother's. If it weren't for my sister Lois, we wouldn't have any at all. Mom was a great cook but she never wrote anything down, so we've had to re-create her recipes from memory with the help of other family members. This one is straight from the source.

4 cups flour

6 teaspoons baking powder

1 teaspoon salt

1 cup sugar

1 cup nuts

2 eggs, beaten

1 cup milk

1. In large bowl, mix together flour, baking powder, salt, sugar, and nuts. Add beaten eggs and milk.
2. Put into 2 greased and floured 9" × 5" × 3" loaf pans and let stand for 20 minutes.
3. Bake at 350° for about 50 minutes.

❧ Makes 2 loaves

Frosty Pumpkin Bread

This is wonderfully good any time of the year, but it's especially good during the holiday season. The icing on this bread is a must.

3⅓ cups flour

1 teaspoon cinnamon

1 teaspoon nutmeg

1 teaspoon cloves

4 eggs

2 cups canned pumpkin

½ cup pecan pieces

2 teaspoons baking soda

1½ teaspoon salt

1 cup vegetable oil

⅔ cup water

3 cups sugar

Icing:

1 teaspoon butter, softened

1 8-ounce package cream cheese, softened

1 16-ounce box of powdered sugar

1 cup of pecans

1 teaspoon vanilla

1. In large bowl, combine all ingredients. Mix well.
2. Grease and flour 3 9" × 5" × 3" loaf pans.
3. Pour mixture into 3 pans.
4. Bake at 350° for 50 to 60 minutes.
5. With electric mixer, beat together butter and cream cheese.
6. Add powdered sugar and beat until smooth.
7. Stir in pecans and vanilla.
8. Frost pumpkin bread while still warm.

Makes 3 loaves

And the house of Israel called the name thereof Manna: and it was like coriander seed, white; and the taste of it was like wafers made with honey.

—Exodus 16:31

Cheese Biscuits

What can we say about cheese biscuits? They're *so* good. Make a batch of these, and they'll be gone before you know it. Best when served warm.

2 cups flour
3 teaspoons baking powder
1 teaspoon salt
¼ cup shortening
⅓ cup shredded Cheddar cheese
1 teaspoon salt
¾ cup milk

1. In a bowl, mix together flour, baking powder, and salt.
2. Cut shortening into flour with pastry blender or fork until it looks like cornmeal.
3. Stir in grated cheese.
4. Add milk to mixture just enough to hold dough together.
5. Roll dough ½" thick.
6. Cut and bake on ungreased cookie sheet at 425° for 12 to 15 minutes.

Makes 16 to 20

Pineapple Nut Bread

This is an impressive and delicious bread that is wonderfully moist and nutty. Don't forget to add the cinnamon mixture as a finishing touch before you put it in the oven.

¾ cup brown sugar
¼ cup shortening
1 egg, beaten
2 cups flour
1 teaspoon baking soda
½ teaspoon salt
3 ounces frozen orange juice concentrate
1 cup crushed pineapple, undrained
½ cup chopped pecans
2 tablespoons sugar
½ teaspoon cinnamon

1. In medium bowl, cream brown sugar and shortening.
2. Add egg.
3. Sift together flour, baking soda, and salt.
4. Add orange juice concentrate and crushed pineapple to creamed mixture.
5. Sift dry ingredients into creamed mixture, blending well.
6. Stir in pecans.

continued

(Pineapple Nut Bread—continued)

7. Pour into 2 greased and floured 9" × 5" × 3" loaf pans.
8. Combine sugar and cinnamon and sprinkle on top of loaves.
9. Bake at 350° for 50 to 60 minutes.

Makes 2 loaves

Thou gavest also thy good spirit to instruct them, and withheldest not thy manna from their mouth, and gavest them water for their thirst.

—Nehemiah 9:20

Garlic Cheese Biscuits

If you like the biscuits at Red Lobster, you'll love Annis's recipe for these garlic cheese biscuits. They're as good as the ones served at the restaurant.

11 ounces cold milk
2¼ cups Bisquick
3 ounces shredded Cheddar cheese
½ cup melted butter
1 teaspoon garlic powder
⅛ teaspoon onion powder
⅛ teaspoon dried parsley flakes

1. To cold milk, add Bisquick and cheese and blend together.
2. Using a small scoop, place dough on greased cookie sheet.
3. Bake at 375° for 10 to 12 minutes or until golden brown.
4. Brush baked biscuits with garlic topping made with butter, garlic powder, onion powder, and parsley.

Makes 12 biscuits

Spiced Applesauce Loaf

This fast and easy bread will appeal to everyone who loves apples. The wonderful smell will bring everyone into the kitchen. You will be tempted to keep it for yourself and your family rather than give it away.

1¼ cups applesauce

1 cup sugar

½ cup cooking oil

2 eggs

3 tablespoons milk

2 cups flour

1 teaspoon baking soda

½ teaspoon baking powder

½ teaspoon cinnamon

¼ teaspoon salt

¼ teaspoon nutmeg

¾ cup chopped pecans

¼ cup brown sugar

½ teaspoon cinnamon

1. Combine applesauce, sugar, oil, eggs, and milk. Mix well.
2. Sift together flour, baking soda, baking powder, cinnamon, salt, and nutmeg.
3. Stir into applesauce mixture and mix well.
4. Fold in ½ cup of the pecans.
5. Place in 2 greased 9" × 5" × 3" loaf pans.
6. Combine the remaining pecans, brown sugar, and cinnamon.
7. Sprinkle over batter.
8. Bake at 350° for 1 hour.
9. Remove from pan and cool.

🍲 Makes 2 loaves

The meek shall eat and be satisfied:
they shall praise the LORD that seek him:
your heart shall live for ever.

—Psalms 22:26

Banana Tea Bread

Don't throw those ripe bananas away. Instead make them into bread. That's what my dear friend Kathi's sister-in-law does with her ripe bananas. Kathi tells me this recipe is wonderful, and so is her sister-in-law Diane.

2 cups sugar

1 cup butter, softened

6 ripe bananas, mashed

4 eggs

2½ cups flour

1 teaspoon salt

2 teaspoons baking soda

1. In a large bowl, cream sugar and butter until fluffy.
2. Add bananas and eggs and blend.
3. Sift together the flour, salt, and soda 3 times.
4. Carefully blend flour mixture into bananas. Do not overmix.
5. Pour into 2 greased 9" × 5" × 3" loaf pans.
6. Bake at 350° for 50 to 55 minutes.
7. Cool for 10 minutes.

ॐ Makes 2 loaves

Lemon Bread

The wonderful glaze on this bread gives it a terrific lemony flavor. This bread will melt in your mouth. It was a favorite at my store and was made by my friend Shirley.

⅔ cup butter

2 cups sugar

4 eggs

3 cups flour

1 cup milk

1 tablespoon baking powder

2 teaspoons salt

1 cup pecan pieces

4 tablespoons lemon juice

⅔ cup sugar

1. Combine all ingredients except lemon juice and sugar. Blend well.
2. Put into 2 greased 9" × 5" × 3" loaf pans.
3. Bake at 350° for 50 to 60 minutes.
4. While breads are still warm, combine lemon juice and sugar.
5. Pour over bread.

ॐ Makes 2 loaves

Pineapple Zucchini Bread

Sometimes the only way to get your children to eat healthy foods is by including them in your recipes. This bread is so delicious that your children won't know they are eating something good for them.

3 eggs, beaten slightly

1 cup vegetable oil

2 teaspoons vanilla extract

2 cups sugar

2 cups grated zucchini

1 teaspoon baking soda

3 cups flour

1 teaspoon salt

1 teaspoon baking powder

1 cup chopped pecans

1 20-ounce can crushed pineapple, drained

2 tablespoons sugar

½ teaspoon cinnamon

1. In a large mixing bowl, mix together eggs, oil, vanilla, sugar, and zucchini.
2. Add baking soda, flour, salt, baking powder, pecans, and drained pineapple.
3. Pour into 2 greased loaf pans.
4. Mix together sugar and cinnamon.
5. Sprinkle over loaves.
6. Bake at 350° for 50 to 60 minutes or until a toothpick inserted near center comes out clean.

Makes 2 loaves

Butter and honey shall he eat, that he may know to refuse the evil, and choose the good.

—Isaiah 7:15

Entrées

Surprise

A few years ago, my sister Lois turned 70 years young. Aside from the birthday anniversary itself, the real story lies in the behind-the-scenes family preparation for that event. For starters, anyone who knew Lois was aware that she was not one to willingly come to a big birthday bash in her honor. Rather, we worried that if she found out about it in advance, she would find a way not to come at all! Therefore, our planning had to be covert, and we promised each other that none of us would spill the beans. This was more than just a family challenge: Lois's friends and coworkers were also to be invited, and just one person could easily and inadvertently spoil the surprise.

Since Lois lives in northern Indiana, we schemers traveled to Indianapolis and met at the local IHOP, about 75 miles from her hometown. The planning then began. After resolving the questions of when, where, and how to celebrate, and who to invite, we sprang into action. We were able to obtain a large activity room in a church that her son Ed and his wife Marilyn attended. Now the question was: How were we going to get Lois to the church activity room on a Saturday afternoon? The answer was to tell her that her grandson had a display project set up there, and she was invited to see it.

During the hours before the surprise party, we carried in food and more food—a bountiful banquet of food, fit for any VIP. Some of us set up the room with balloons and other birthday trimmings while the rest of us set up the buffet. As Lois's friends and other family members arrived, they went into the activity room to prepare for the big surprise.

continued

We all remained silent as Ed drove Lois into the church parking lot and entered the entrance hallway with her. Then Lois entered the activity room and we let loose with our shouts of "SURPRISE!" She *was* surprised—not a hint had been dropped to give us away. And there was no escaping for Lois now—Ed was right behind her to block the doorway.

As it turned out, she had a great time, and I know she was really pleased that all of her friends and family came together to show her how much she meant to us. Plan a party for one of your friends or relatives. Even shy and modest people like to be feted. Use some of the recipes in this book to keep things easy and delicious. ◖

Open-Faced Stroganoff Loaf

You can make this loaf ahead of time and freeze it for when you need to take something unexpectedly. It is perfect to take to a family in time of need, as they can use it immediately or freeze it for later use. Thanks, Vicki, for sharing this recipe with me.

1½ pounds ground beef
½ cup chopped onion
1 cup water
½ cup sour cream
1 1.5-ounce envelope stroganoff seasoning mix
1 loaf Vienna bread, unsliced
Butter
1 green pepper, sliced in rings
Cherry tomatoes, halved
1 4.5-ounce can sliced mushrooms, drained

1. Brown meat and onion. Drain well.
2. Stir in water, sour cream, and seasoning mix.
3. Cover and simmer 10 minutes.
4. Cut bread in half lengthwise. Butter bread and top with meat mixture.
5. Arrange green peppers and tomatoes alternately.
6. Place mushrooms on top.
7. Bake at 375° for 7 to 10 minutes.
8. Wrap in foil to keep warm.

 Serves 10 to 12

Spanish Rice

My brother-in-law's mother, Eva, made the best Spanish rice I ever tasted. I still remember going over to her home for dinner and eating way too much of it. Unfortunately, I never did get her recipe for it. This is the closest I've come to finding one as delicious as hers.

1 pound ground beef
1 pound sausage
1 tablespoon vegetable oil
1½ cups chopped onions
1½ cups chopped green pepper
2 cups rice
2 cups hot water
2 8-ounce cans diced tomatoes
2 10.75-ounce cans tomato soup
2 tablespoons paprika

1. Cook ground beef and sausage until brown. Drain well on paper towels.
2. In same skillet, heat oil and cook onions and green pepper for 2 to 3 minutes. Add ground beef and sausage to onions and peppers.
3. In large saucepan, mix together remaining ingredients. Add beef mixture. Cook on medium heat until sauce thickens and rice is tender, usually 20 to 30 minutes.
4. Top with sour cream, shredded cheese, or other favorite condiments.

Serves 10 to 12

Reuben Casserole

Who doesn't like a good Reuben sandwich? Be sure to buy your corned beef for this dish from the deli, as it really makes a difference. Also, I rinse the sauerkraut a couple of times with cold water so it won't be quite so salty.

2 cups sauerkraut, drained
1 cup sour cream
1 pound deli chipped corned beef
3 cups shredded Swiss cheese
8 slices rye bread
½ cup butter
Thousand Island dressing

1. Mix together sauerkraut and sour cream.
2. Spread in bottom of 9" × 13" greased baking dish.
3. Spread corned beef over sauerkraut mixture.
4. Put cheese on top of corned beef.
5. Break bread into pieces and put on top of cheese.
6. Pour melted butter on top and bake at 350° for 30 minutes.
7. Serve with Thousand Island dressing.

 Serves 8 to 10

Tostada Pie

My sister Marilyn made this when we were visiting her and her husband, Paul, in Las Vegas. She shared this recipe with me and I made it for a carry-in as soon as we arrived back home. I was glad I took the recipe along, as several others wanted to have it as well.

Vegetable cooking spray
1 8-ounce tube crescent rolls
1½ pounds ground beef
¾ cup mild salsa
¾ cup medium salsa
1 cup sour cream
1 16-ounce can refried beans
1 cup Mexican blend shredded cheese
½ cup sliced black olives
½ cup chopped tomatoes
¼ cup sliced green onions

1. Preheat oven to 375°.
2. Spray 9" pie pan with vegetable cooking spray.
3. Press crescent rolls into pie plate to form crust.
4. Brown meat and drain well.
5. In bowl, combine ground beef, salsas, and sour cream.
6. Spread refried beans onto crescent rolls.
7. Put ground beef mixture on top of refried beans.
8. Top with cheese, olives, tomatoes, and onions.
9. Bake for 15 minutes or until cheese is melted.

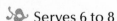 Serves 6 to 8

Five-Hour Barbecue

My sister-in-law Gayle gave me her friend Ruth's recipe for this barbecue. When Gayle was telling me how good Ruth's was she quickly added that mine was a favorite of hers as well. (I tried Ruth's and it might be even better than mine!) As barbecue is one of my favorites, I find it difficult to pick my most favorite out of all the recipes that are in this cookbook.

2 tablespoons vinegar

2 tablespoons Worcestershire sauce

1 tablespoon salt

¼ teaspoon red pepper

½ teaspoon black pepper

1 teaspoon paprika

1 teaspoon chili powder

1 8-ounce bottle of ketchup

2 cups water

2 medium onions, chopped

1 5-ounce can tomato sauce

3 pounds chuck or rump roast

1. Mix together all ingredients but the last.
2. Pour over meat.
3. Bake covered at 325° for 5 hours.
4. Drain off any grease from sauce.
5. Shred with 2 forks.
6. Serve on fresh buns with cole slaw.

🍃 Makes 12 sandwiches

Open-Faced Reuben

I used to make a stuffed Reuben loaf from a recipe given to me by my friend and former coworker, Gwen. I have lost track of her, but I still remember how good her stuffed loaves were. I now make this one instead, as it is simpler and a bit less time-consuming.

1 loaf Italian or French bread

4 tablespoons butter

½ cup Thousand Island dressing

1½ pounds thinly sliced corned beef

1 16-ounce can sauerkraut, drained

2 cups shredded Swiss cheese

Thousand Island dressing

1. Preheat oven to 375°.
2. Slice bread lengthwise and butter both pieces.
3. Spread dressing on both pieces.
4. Top each piece with layers of corned beef, sauerkraut, and cheese.
5. Bake for 7 to 10 minutes until cheese melts.
6. Wrap in foil.
7. Cut in pieces when ready to serve.
8. Serve with extra Thousand Island dressing.

🍃 Makes 16 pieces

Baked Beef Stew

When I mentioned I was writing another cookbook, my friend Sally was kind enough to share this and a few other favorite recipes. This one may take 3 hours to bake, but it only takes 5 minutes of your time to prepare.

3 pounds lean stew beef
1 2-ounce package onion soup mix
2 10.75-ounce cans golden-mushroom soup
½ cup Sauterne wine

1. Combine all ingredients and place in 9" × 13" greased baking dish.
2. Cover with foil.
3. Bake at 300° for 3 hours.

Serves 8 to 10

Take thou also unto thee wheat, and barley, and beans, and lentiles, and millet, and fitches, and put them in one vessel, and make thee bread thereof, according to the number of the days that thou shalt lie upon thy side, three hundred and ninety days shalt thou eat thereof.

—Ezekiel 4:9

Beef Barbecue

This recipe can be fixed in a Crock-Pot, shortening the time you need to fix it and making it very easy to take to any event. This is my sister Anita's recipe, re-created to taste as much like Mom's as we can remember. The sauce has been changed a little as it's been handed down through the years by many a good cook in our family.

3 pounds beef stew meat
¼ cup broth from cooking beef
½ cup Montgomery Inn barbecue sauce
1 cup ketchup
½ teaspoon Worcestershire sauce
2 tablespoons brown sugar

1. Put beef in pan and cover with water.
2. Cook on top of stove for 2 to 3 hours or until tender.
3. Drain liquid, reserving ¼ cup for sauce.
4. Shred beef with fork or a potato masher.
5. Add broth and remaining ingredients.
6. Heat and serve on buns.

Serves 12 to 15

Braised Chuck Rosemary

I received this recipe in 1970 when my husband was in the Navy. One of the other Navy wives, Pam, brought it to one of our monthly gatherings while our husbands were out to sea. I lost track of Pam and no doubt she has forgotten me, but I still use her tasty recipe.

Vegetable cooking spray

4 to 5 pounds beef rump roast

1 cup sliced onion rings

1 teaspoon minced jarred garlic

½ cup ketchup

½ teaspoon rosemary

½ cup water

¼ cup red wine vinegar

2 tablespoons Worcestershire sauce

1 teaspoon dry mustard

3 pounds peeled white potatoes

1. Brown meat well on both sides in a heavy pan sprayed with vegetable cooking spray.
2. Add onion and garlic, and cook until onions are tender.
3. Combine remaining ingredients except potatoes.
4. Pour over meat.
5. Cover and cook slowly over medium heat until meat is fork tender, about 2½ hours.
6. Drop potatoes around roast and cook for 25 minutes.
7. Cover and cook till potatoes are done.

Serves 12 to 15

Brunswick Stew

My friend Sally, who gave me this recipe, tells me that this is really her dad, Pap's, recipe. It seems that a number of years ago, they were at a football game in Williamsburg, Virginia. They went into a restaurant and ordered the Brunswick Stew. Her dad went home and re-created the recipe—he was able to tell what ingredients were in it just from eating it.

3 medium potatoes, pared and cut in ½" pieces

1 10-ounce package frozen baby lima beans

1 10-ounce package frozen okra

1 10-ounce package frozen corn

3 cups cooked chicken, diced

1 tablespoon sugar

1 teaspoon salt

½ teaspoon rosemary

Dash pepper

⅛ teaspoon cloves

1 bay leaf

4 cups chicken broth

1 16-ounce can tomatoes

1. Place potatoes and frozen vegetables in a Crock-Pot.
2. Add chicken, sugar, salt, rosemary, pepper, cloves, and bay leaf.

continued

3. Pour chicken broth and undrained tomatoes over mixture.
4. Cover and cook on low heat setting for 8 to 10 hours.
5. Remove bay leaf and stir well.

Serves 10

And thou shalt rejoice in thy feast, thou, and thy son, and thy daughter, and thy manser-vant, and thy maidservant, and the Levite, the stranger, and the fatherless, and the widow, that are within thy gates.

—Deuteronomy 16:14

Cabbage Roll Casserole

Cabbage rolls are a little time-consuming to make, but doesn't everyone love them. Sally says this casserole is a snap to make.

1 small head of cabbage
1 pound ground beef or turkey
Salt and pepper
½ tablespoon minced garlic
1 small onion, diced
⅓ cup rice, uncooked
1 16-ounce can sauerkraut
1 8-ounce can tomato sauce
1½ cups water

1. Chop cabbage into bite-size pieces and place in greased 9" × 13" pan.
2. Brown meat, drain, and add salt, pepper, garlic, and onion.
3. Scatter rice over cabbage.
4. Pour meat mixture over cabbage and rice.
5. Cover with sauerkraut, tomato sauce, and water.
6. Bake uncovered at 350° for 20 minutes.
7. Cover and continue baking for another hour or until rice is tender.

Makes 8 to 10

Estofado

I was so pleased that Jean was willing to share this wonderfully different dish. She has prepared it for her dinner club friends, one of whom mentioned it to me. Isn't that the way it is—good recipes get passed around and around. Thank heavens.

3 pounds lean beef, cut in 1" cubes

1 tablespoon cooking oil

1 cup dry red wine

1 8-ounce can tomatoes

1 large onion, sliced ¼" thick

1 green pepper, cut in strips

¼ cup raisins

¼ cup dried apricots, halved

½ teaspoon jarred minced garlic

1½ teaspoons salt

⅛ teaspoon pepper

1 recipe bouquet garni (see below)

½ cup sliced fresh mushrooms

¼ cup sliced ripe olives

1 tablespoon flour

1 cup cold water

Hot cooked rice

1. In large skillet, brown meat in hot oil.

2. Add wine, tomatoes, onion, green pepper, raisins, apricots, garlic, salt, and pepper.
3. Make bouquet garni by tying together in cheesecloth 1 teaspoon dried basil, 1 teaspoon dried thyme, 1 teaspoon dried tarragon, and 1 bay leaf.
4. Simmer, covered, for 1 hour.
5. Add mushrooms and olives.
6. Simmer for 30 minutes.
7. Discard bouquet garni.
8. Combine flour and cold water and stir into stew.
9. Cook, stirring constantly, until mixture thickens and bubbles.
10. Serve over rice.

Serves 12

And they shall eat up thine harvest, and thy bread, which thy sons and thy daughters should eat: they shall eat up thy flocks and thine herds: they shall eat up thy vines and thy fig trees: they shall impoverish thy fenced cities, wherein thou trustedst, with the sword.

—Jeremiah 5:17

Lasagna

I remember how nervous I was when my husband, Larry, and I went to his boss' house for dinner the first time. I certainly needn't have been, as Wendy and Terry made us feel right at home and eased my nervousness pretty quickly. Wendy had prepared lasagna and her recipe immediately became one of my most treasured ones. I have made it countless times and it is always a hit.

1½ 8-ounce boxes lasagna noodles

2 tablespoons vegetable oil

1½ pounds lean ground beef

¼ teaspoon pepper

2 cups spaghetti sauce (I use 1 package French's mix—using the tomato paste alternative, it makes exactly 2 cups)

1 16-ounce container small curd cottage cheese

¼ cup sour cream

2 8-ounce packages mozzarella cheese slices

Vegetable oil

1. Cook noodles as package directs. Drain.
2. Toss with 2 tablespoons vegetable oil until well coated.
3. In skillet, brown ground beef and drain very well.
4. Add pepper and spaghetti sauce and stir well.
5. Combine cottage cheese with sour cream.
6. Arrange half of noodles in 9" × 13" greased baking dish.
7. Cover with half of meat sauce mixture.
8. Add layer of cheese slices (using ½ total cheese).
9. Add all cottage cheese–sour cream mixture.
10. Top with remaining noodles.
11. Add rest of mozzarella cheese cut into ½" strips, laid lattice fashion across the top.
12. Spoon remaining meat-sauce mixture into lattice spaces.
13. Cover tightly and refrigerate until ready to bake.
14. Heat oven to 350°.
15. Brush surface of cheese strips with vegetable oil.
16. Bake 30 minutes or until cheese melts and is golden.

Serves 8 to 10

My meat also which I gave thee, fine flour, and oil, and honey, wherewith I fed thee, thou hast even set it before them for a sweet savour: and thus it was, saith the Lord GOD.

—Ezekiel 16:19

Crustless Pizza Pie

If you're hungry for pizza and you're in a hurry, try this pizza recipe that Annis shared with me. You could also use chopped pepperoni and green peppers on top of the ground beef to make a supreme pizza.

1½ pounds ground beef
¾ teaspoon pepper
1½ cups well-drained canned tomatoes
3 tablespoons chopped parsley
⅜ teaspoon dried basil
1½ teaspoons garlic powder
3 tablespoons finely chopped onion
¼ teaspoon oregano
¾ cup shredded Mozzarella cheese

1. Mix ground beef with salt and pepper.
2. Pat out in a 9" pie pan.
3. Spread drained tomatoes over ground beef and sprinkle with remaining ingredients.
4. Bake at 375° for 15 to 20 minutes.
5. Cut in wedges and serve.

 Serves 6

Reuben Roll-Ups

When you're making these, be sure to take along a bottle or a container of Thousand Island dressing. I like to drizzle just a little over my roll-up. Another easy one from Annis.

1 8-ounce package refrigerator crescent rolls
8 thin slices of deli corned beef
1 8-ounce can sauerkraut, drained
2 tablespoons Thousand Island dressing
2 slices Swiss cheese, cut in ½" strips

1. Preheat oven to 350°.
2. Unroll crescent rolls and separate into triangles.
3. Place a slice of corned beef across wide end of each triangle.
4. Combine sauerkraut with salad dressing.
5. Spread 2 tablespoons of mixture on corned beef.
6. Top with 2 strips of cheese.
7. Roll up, beginning at wide end of triangle, and place on an ungreased baking sheet.
8. Bake for 10 to 15 minutes or until golden brown.
9. Remove from oven and slice each into thirds.
10. Serve warm or cold.

 Serves 8

Shepherd's Pie

This meat pie is a classic dish that can be made with instant mashed potatoes if you're in a hurry. It won't be quite as good, but it will take less of your time.

2 chopped onions

1 pound ground beef

2 tablespoons ketchup

¼ teaspoon Worcestershire sauce

1 16-ounce bag frozen mixed vegetables, thawed

4 to 6 cups mashed potatoes

¼ cup milk

3 tablespoons butter

Dash salt

1. Brown onions and ground beef together in large skillet. Drain well.
2. Add ketchup, Worcestershire sauce, and vegetables.
3. Pour into greased 8" × 8" square baking dish.
4. Beat together potatoes, milk, butter, and salt.
5. Spread over filling. Seal to edge.
6. Bake at 425° for 35 minutes.

Serves 6 to 8

Judee's Sloppy Joes

Judee gave me this recipe and told me it was one of her "quickie" recipes. She was right. These sloppy joes are much quicker to prepare than the ones you make on the top of your stove. You do have to remember to stir them about every 20 or 30 minutes. But it beats standing over a hot stove browning your ground beef when you could be doing something else.

2 pounds ground beef

1 cup chopped onion

½ cup chopped green pepper

1 10.75-ounce can mushroom soup

½ 10.75-ounce can tomato soup

¾ cup ketchup

½ teaspoon prepared mustard

Dash Worcestershire sauce

1. Mix all ingredients together.
2. Put in greased 9" × 13" baking dish.
3. Bake at 350° for 1½ hours, stirring occasionally.
4. Pour off grease on top, if any.

Serves 8 to 10

Stroganoff Steak Sandwich

This comes from a dear "old" friend, Sharon. She may be aging chronologically (like the rest of us), but she still has the same young spirit she had when we were neighbors in Virginia back in the early '70s. We shared a love of cooking as well as a wonderful friendship. I've wished many times that I was again living close to my dear friend. Thank heavens for memories.

⅔ cup beer

⅓ cup cooking oil

1 teaspoon salt

¼ teaspoon garlic powder

¼ teaspoon pepper

2 pounds flank steak, 1" thick

2 tablespoons margarine or butter

½ teaspoon paprika

Dash salt

4 cups sliced onion

12 slices French bread, toasted

1 cup sour cream, warmed

½ teaspoon prepared horseradish

Paprika

1. In shallow dish, combine first 5 ingredients.
2. Place flank steak in marinade; cover.
3. Marinate overnight in refrigerator or several hours at room temperature.
4. Drain.
5. Broil flank steak 3" from heat for 5 to 7 minutes for medium-rare.
6. In saucepan, melt margarine and blend in paprika and dash salt.
7. Add onion. Cook till tender but not brown.
8. Thinly slice meat on the diagonal across grain.
9. For each serving, arrange meat slices over 2 slices French bread.
10. Top with onions.
11. Combine sour cream and horseradish.
12. Spoon onto each sandwich.
13. Sprinkle with paprika if desired.

Serves 6

And Boaz said unto her, At mealtime come thou hither, and eat of the bread, and dip thy morsel in the vinegar. And she sat beside the reapers: and he reached her parched corn, and she did eat, and was sufficed, and left.

—Ruth 2:14

Taco Salad

When I need something in a hurry I make this salad, and take along a bag of tortilla chips to add when it's time to serve. You can mix the dressing in a small container and take it along as well. It's my "take-out" salad.

1 pound ground beef

1 head lettuce

1 cup chopped onions

2 cups diced tomatoes

1 cup grated Cheddar cheese

5 ounces (½ 10-ounce package) tortilla chips

1 cup French dressing

¼ cup mayonnaise

¼ to ½ cup salsa

1. Brown ground beef in skillet. Drain on paper towels to remove grease.
2. Tear lettuce apart and put into large bowl.
3. On top of lettuce, put meat, onions, tomatoes, cheese, and chips.
4. Mix together French dressing, mayonnaise, and salsa and pour over salad when ready to serve. Toss well.

Serves 6 to 8

Barbecue Cups (Fu Manchu on Sundays)

When my kids were around ten and eleven, my sister Lois came to visit with her son Joe, also eleven. All of them were finicky about what they ate, so my sister and I decided to fix these barbecue cups, not sure whether they would eat them. Consequently, we came up with the name "Fu Manchu on Sundays" when they kept asking us what we were having. It became quite a game. The kids loved them, and I think it was thanks to our silliness and the fun we had.

1 pound ground beef

½ cup chopped onion

Salt and pepper to taste

1 tablespoon brown sugar

¼ cup bottled barbecue sauce

1 7.5-ounce tube refrigerated biscuits

1. Brown ground beef and onion.
2. Pour off excess fat.
3. Add seasoning and sugar and barbecue sauce.
4. Simmer for 5 minutes.
5. Separate biscuits.
6. Press into bottom and sides of a greased muffin tin.
7. Fill with meat mixture and top with cheese.
8. Bake at 400° for 10 to 15 minutes.

Serves 8

Meat Loaf

This is Kim's meat loaf recipe and our family's favorite meat loaf. Kim, a single mom, raised her son all on her own. Having gone through many rough times in her life, she is a true survivor. I'm proud to know this hardworking, God-loving woman, and honored to be her friend.

Meatloaf:

2 pounds ground beef

1 pound ground pork

1 tablespoon Worcestershire sauce

1 teaspoon garlic

¼ cup minced onion

2 sleeves saltines, crushed

2 eggs

¾ cup ketchup

Sauce:

¾ cup brown sugar

2 tablespoons Worcestershire sauce

¾ to 1 cup ketchup

1. Mix together meat loaf ingredients.
2. Divide in half and put in 2 greased 9" × 5" × 3" loaf pans.
3. Bake at 350° for 35 to 45 minutes.
4. In small bowl, combine sauce ingredients.
5. Remove from oven, poke holes on top with fork, and cover with sauce.
6. Put back in oven for 10 to 20 minutes until sauce is bubbly.

Makes 2 loaves

And ye shall offer with the bread seven lambs without blemish of the first year, and one young bullock, and two rams: they shall be for a burnt offering unto the LORD, with their meat offering, and their drink offerings, even an offering made by fire, of sweet savour unto the LORD.

—Leviticus 23:18

Chicken Quiche

Good for breakfast, lunch, or dinner!

1/8 teaspoon white pepper

1 pound boneless, skinless chicken breasts, cut into
    bite-size pieces

1/4 cup vegetable oil

1 large peeled onion, thinly sliced and separated into rings

1 large tomato, peeled, seeded, cubed, and drained

3 eggs

3/4 cup milk

3/4 cup half-and-half

3/4 cup Gruyère cheese

1/4 cup Parmesan cheese

1 10" partially baked pastry shell

1 teaspoon butter

1. Preheat oven to 375°. Sprinkle pepper over
   chicken.
2. Sauté chicken in oil for 5 to 6 minutes. Set aside.
3. Add onion rings to skillet and cook over medium
   low heat until tender.
4. Add tomato. Cook until tender.
5. Beat eggs and add milk, half-and-half, and
   cheeses.
6. Arrange onion, tomato, and chicken in pie shell
   and pour egg mixture over all. Dot with butter.
7. Bake at 375° for 35 to 40 minutes in the upper
   part of the oven.

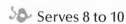 Serves 8 to 10

Chicken-Spinach Roll-Ups

This is one of those quick recipes to fix when you're
having a hectic day. It doesn't take long to prepare,
and you can take a few minutes to unwind while it's
baking in the oven. I was delighted when my sister
Anita shared this delicious recipe with me.

Vegetable cooking spray

2 10.75-ounce cans cream of chicken soup

2 cups sour cream

4 tablespoons Dijonnaise

1 cup minute rice

2 cups small curd cottage cheese

2 eggs

1/2 cup chopped onion

1/2 cup flour

1 10-ounce package chopped spinach, thawed and
    drained

20 slices deli chicken breast

1/2 cup breadcrumbs

1. Preheat oven to 350°.
2. In small bowl, combine soup, sour cream, and
   Dijonnaise.
3. In a medium-size bowl, mix half of the soup mixture with the rice, cottage cheese, eggs, onion,
   flour, and spinach.

continued

4. Place 2 tablespoons of the mixture on each slice of chicken breast. Spread mixture with spoon and roll up.
5. Spray 11" × 17" baking dish with vegetable cooking spray. Placing seam side down, put chicken rolls in dish.
6. Top with remaining soup mixture and bread crumbs.
7. Bake for 30 to 35 minutes.

Serves 10

And Solomon gave Hiram twenty thousand measures of wheat for food to his household, and twenty measures of pure oil: thus gave Solomon to Hiram year by year.

—1 Kings 5:11

Cranberry Chicken

I know this combination of cranberry sauce and Catalina dressing, along with the onion soup mix, seems pretty strange. But those of you who are familiar with the recipe using Russian dressing and onion soup mix will also like this one.

10 boneless skinless chicken breasts
1 16-ounce can whole-berry cranberry sauce
1 16-ounce bottle Catalina dressing
1 2-ounce package dry onion soup mix
Rice

1. Place chicken breasts in a greased 9" × 13" baking dish.
2. Mix together cranberry sauce, dressing, and onion soup mix.
3. Pour mixture over chicken breasts.
4. Cover with foil and bake at 350° for 50 to 60 minutes.
5. Uncover and bake 15 minutes more.
6. Serve with rice.

Serves 10

Dill Rice Chicken

Jenny, my friend Kathi's daughter, just made Kathi a proud Granny for the first time. Jenny's friend Wendy made this for her after she brought little Sarah home. Take it to a friend of yours who has a newborn—she'll be thrilled.

1 cup sour cream

1 10.75-ounce can cream of chicken soup

1 10.75-ounce can cream of mushroom soup

1 16-ounce bag frozen vegetables, thawed

3 cups cooked chicken

3 cups cooked rice

1 teaspoon poppy seed

1¼ teaspoons dill weed

¼ teaspoon onion salt

¼ teaspoon garlic salt

1 cup shredded Cheddar cheese

Vegetable cooking spray

1. In a large bowl, mix together all ingredients.
2. Spray 9" × 14" baking dish with vegetable cooking spray.
3. Place chicken mixture in dish.
4. Bake at 350° for 30 minutes.
5. If desired, add crushed crackers on top in the last 10 minutes.

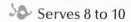 Serves 8 to 10

Chicken à la Ritz

The Ritz crackers on this chicken dish give it just the right crunch. Surprise one of your busy friends with this dish for dinner. You'll make her day!

10 chicken breasts

2 10.75-ounce cans cream of chicken soup

1 cup sour cream

32 Ritz crackers, crushed

2 teaspoons poppy seeds

6 tablespoons melted butter

1. Cut chicken into bite-size pieces.
2. Place in greased 9" × 13" baking dish.
3. Mix together soup and sour cream and pour over chicken.
4. Sprinkle crackers on top and then poppy seeds on top of crackers.
5. Drizzle butter over crackers.
6. Bake at 350° uncovered for 30 to 40 minutes, until bubbly around the sides.
7. Serve over rice if desired.

Serves 8 to 10

Chicken-Asparagus Supreme

This is especially great with fresh asparagus. If you use fresh, be sure to precook it for about 5 to 10 minutes before putting it in the baking dish. It's also good with white asparagus.

2 8-ounce packages of frozen asparagus spears, drained and cooked
5 cups cooked cut-up chicken
2 10.75-ounce cans cream of chicken soup
1 cup mayonnaise
1 teaspoon lemon juice
8 ounces shredded Cheddar cheese
1 cup corn flake crumbs
Butter

1. Cover bottom of greased 9" × 13" casserole dish with asparagus spears.
2. Cover asparagus with cut-up chicken.
3. Mix soup with mayonnaise and lemon juice.
4. Pour mixture over chicken.
5. Sprinkle top with grated cheese.
6. Top with corn flake crumbs and dot generously with butter.
7. Bake at 350° for 30 minutes or until golden brown and bubbly.

Serves 8 to 10

Georgia's Fried Chicken

Talk about fried chicken! This is by far the best fried chicken I have ever tasted—and I've had a lot of different fried chicken. When Georgia makes her chicken, she always calls me to come over and try a piece or two. I drop whatever I am doing and go.

Pure canola oil
15 chicken legs
3 cups flour
Black pepper
Salt

1. Heat griddle to 400°.
2. Add ½" canola oil.
3. Rinse and drain chicken legs.
4. Put flour into large paper sack and shake chicken legs in flour.
5. Place one piece of chicken at a time onto the griddle.
6. Shake a little salt and pepper on the up side of the chicken.
7. When the first side is lightly browned, approximately 10 minutes, turn the chicken over and sprinkle with salt and pepper on the new up side.
8. Fry to a golden tan for about 45 minutes, turning chicken over about every 10 minutes to keep from burning.
9. Drain on paper towels.

Makes 15

Homemade Chicken Pot Pie

If you love old-fashioned cooking but don't think you have the time to fix it, try this recipe. This pot pie comes close to the old version, but will take little time to prepare.

1 2/3 cups frozen mixed vegetables, thawed
1 cup cooked chicken, cut into bite-size pieces
1 10.75-ounce can cream of chicken soup
1 cup Bisquick original baking mix
1/2 cup milk
1 egg

1. Preheat oven to 400°.
2. Mix together vegetables, chicken, and soup in an ungreased 9" pie plate.
3. Stir remaining ingredients with fork until blended.
4. Pour over chicken mixture.
5. Bake at 400° for 30 minutes or until golden brown.

Serves 6

Chicken Jewel

The young lady, Lauren, who has been helping me with my book brought this recipe from her soon-to-be mother-in-law, Linda. I went to the grocery right away and put this together in a matter of minutes. My daughter Joelle came in as I was taking it out of the oven and we all had a taste test. She liked it so much she took at least half of it home with her.

2 10-ounce cans of chicken breast, drained
1/2 cup chopped onion
1 1/2 cups shredded Cheddar cheese
2 cups crushed Nacho Cheese Doritos
1 10.75-ounce can cream of mushroom soup
1 10.75-ounce can cream of chicken soup
1 14.5-ounce can Rotel tomatoes and green chilies
1 can water

1. In a greased 9" x 13" pan, place shredded chicken on the bottom.
2. Put onions on top of chicken.
3. Sprinkle 1/2 cup of the cheese on top of onion.
4. Put crushed Doritos on top of cheese.
5. On the stove, over medium heat, mix together and cook soups, tomatoes, and water.
6. Pour on top of Doritos.
7. Sprinkle remaining 1 cup of cheese on top.
8. Bake in the oven at 350° for 30 to 45 minutes until bubbly and crust forms on top.

Serves 8 to 10

Chicken Oriental

French-fried onion rings, water chestnuts, and almonds give this dish a nice, crunchy taste. You can substitute chow mein noodles to give it more of an oriental twist, if you like.

¾ cup mayonnaise

2 teaspoons soy sauce

2 tablespoons lemon juice

Vegetable cooking spray

1 cup diced onion

1½ cups thinly sliced celery

6 thinly sliced mushrooms

4 cups cooked chicken, diced

1 8-ounce can water chestnuts, drained

¼ cup slivered almonds

1 3-ounce can French-fried onion rings

1. Preheat oven to 350°.
2. Combine mayonnaise, soy sauce, and lemon juice. Mix well.
3. Spray skillet with cooking spray.
4. Add onions, celery, and mushrooms, and sauté until tender for about 10 minutes.
5. Stir in chicken, water chestnuts, and almonds.
6. Put into mayonnaise mixture.
7. Place in greased 8" × 8" baking dish.
8. Bake for 30 minutes. Sprinkle with onion rings. Bake 5 to 10 minutes more.

Serves 6

"Lake Laura" Spaghetti

My cousin Barbara tells me that this recipe was "thrown together" by her mother-in-law Dorothea's dear friend while in search of something for dinner for her three visiting sons. They were at their summer home in Lake Laura, Wisconsin, hence the name. Barb loves the dish as well as the story.

1 lb. spaghetti

1 pound ground turkey

1 pound bacon, cut into thirds

1 pound longhorn cheese sliced or grated

Black pepper

1 14.50-ounce can tomatoes

2 10.75-ounce cans tomato soup

1 12-ounce can tomato paste

1 onion

1. Cook spaghetti according to directions on package. Drain well.
2. Cook ground turkey and bacon separately.
3. In a large bowl mix everything together. Mix well.
4. Pour mixture into 9" × 13" baking dish and bake at 350° for 40 minutes.
5. Serve with Parmesan cheese.

Serves 6 to 8

Chicken on Chipped Beef

My niece Janene gave me this dish that she fondly remembers her mom, Anita, making for her and the rest of the family. Of all the meals I had eaten of my sister's I didn't remember this one. But like everything else Anita makes, it is very good.

1 2.25-ounce jar dried beef

8 boneless, skinless chicken breasts

8 strips bacon

1 16-ounce container sour cream

1 10.75-ounce can cream of mushroom soup

1. Line the bottom of a 9" x 13" pan with chipped dried beef.
2. Wrap boneless chicken breasts with strips of raw bacon.
3. In a bowl, mix sour cream and mushroom soup and pour over chicken.
4. Bake at 275° for 3 hours. Cover with foil for the first hour and a half; remove foil for remaining hour and a half.

🍴 Serves 8 to 10

Alpine Chicken

When a group of Friends volunteers were doing the mailing for our Beavercreek Friends of the Library group at Bobbie's (the current president's) home last March, she gave me this family favorite of hers. I was delighted to get it. Bobbie is a wonderful hostess—she always has homemade cookies for us and makes us feel welcome in her home.

4 cups cooked chicken, cut up

2 cups celery

2 cups bread crumbs

½ cup milk or broth

1 8-ounce package shredded Swiss cheese

1 cup Miracle Whip

¼ cup chopped onion

1 teaspoon salt

1 teaspoon pepper

¼ cup slivered almonds

1. Mix together all ingredients except almonds. Sprinkle almonds on top.
2. Pour into greased 9" x 13" baking dish.
3. Bake 40 minutes at 350°.

🍴 Serves 8 to 10

Honey Mustard Chicken

Janene and Ron tell me that this is always a hit with the adults as well as the kids. Make plenty—it'll disappear quickly. It is good served at room temperature.

¼ cup light mayonnaise

¼ cup Dijonnaise

2 tablespoons honey

¼ teaspoon salt

2 pounds chicken tenders

2 cups corn flakes or crushed crackers

Vegetable cooking spray

1. Preheat oven to 350°.
2. In medium bowl, combine mayonnaise, Dijonnaise, honey, and salt.
3. Coat chicken with above mixture and roll in crumbs.
4. Spray 9" × 13" baking dish with vegetable cooking spray.
5. Place coated chicken in baking dish.
6. Bake at 350° for 1 hour.
7. Test for doneness.

Serves 8 to 10

Turkey Fettuccine

Most of the recipes in this book are easy and quick to prepare. This one can be prepared with chicken or ham or both. If you have a vegetarian in the family, try fixing it with mushrooms and artichoke hearts instead of meat.

1 pound turkey

½ cup chopped onion

½ cup chopped green pepper

1 8-ounce package cream cheese, cubed

1 10.75-ounce can cream of celery soup

½ cup water

½ cup milk

¼ teaspoon garlic salt

2 cups cooked fettuccine

½ cup Parmesan cheese

1. Brown turkey, onion, and green pepper in a large skillet until turkey is done.
2. Drain any grease.
3. Stir in cream cheese, soup, water, milk, and garlic salt.
4. Add noodles.
5. Simmer over medium heat for about 10 minutes.
6. Put mixture into greased 9" × 13" baking dish.
7. Sprinkle with Parmesan cheese.
8. Bake for 20 to 30 minutes.

Serves 8 to 10

Chicken-Broccoli Casserole

When I stopped at Sally's home to drop off some articles for our Friends of the Library newsletter, she offered to share some recipes with me. I was impressed by the way she had them all organized in her computer and the manner in which she had them filed. And her recipes are as good as her organizational skills.

16 ounces cream cheese

2 cups milk

1½ teaspoons garlic powder

½ teaspoon salt

5 chicken breasts

3 16-ounce packages frozen chopped broccoli, thawed

1 cup Parmesan

1. Simmer cream cheese, milk, garlic powder, and salt on low heat until smooth.
2. Boil chicken until done, about 20-30 minutes.
3. Chop chicken into 1" pieces.
4. Cook broccoli for 3 to 5 minutes and drain.
5. Combine chicken and broccoli.
6. Add ½ cup Parmesan cheese and sauce.
7. Put mixture into 9" × 13" baking dish and top with ½ cup Parmesan.
8. Bake covered at 350° for 25 to 30 minutes.

Serves 12

Bride's Never-Fail Company Chicken

I met Ellen for the first time in February of 2005 while attending a dear friend's funeral and discovered that we both shared a love of good food and a love of cooking. Not too much later, I received a surprise package in the mail from her with some good old southern recipes, including this incredible one.

8 to 10 pieces of chicken, either cut-up pieces or chicken breasts

8 to 10 slices Swiss cheese

1 10.75-ounce can cream of chicken soup

¼ cup cooking white wine

½ package or more Pepperidge Farm Original Stuffing Mix

¼ cup melted margarine

1. Grease a baking dish that will accommodate the pieces lying flat.
2. Lay a slice of cheese over the top of each piece of chicken.
3. Mix soup and wine and spoon over chicken and cheese.
4. Spread the stuffing over the top of the chicken.
5. Drizzle the melted margarine over the stuffing.
6. Bake at 360° for 30 to 40 minutes for boneless pieces, 45 to 55 minutes for chicken with bones.

Serves 8 to 10

Chicken-Artichoke Casserole

I was surprised and delighted when I received Laura and Ralph's family and friends' cookbook selection of recipes. We met Ralph and Linda through our local Friends of the Library group. This recipe was taken from their collection and was a recipe of another library member, Carolyn. I really appreciated the thoughtfulness as well as the cookbook.

4 whole chicken breasts, skinless and cut into bite-size pieces
1 teaspoon paprika
½ cup butter
1 cup chopped onion
15 large mushrooms, sliced
2 16-ounce cans artichoke hearts in marinade
1 teaspoon tarragon
1½ tablespoons butter
1½ tablespoons flour
2 cups chicken broth
¼ cup sherry

1. Season chicken with paprika.
2. In large skillet, sauté onion in butter and add mushrooms.
3. Add chicken to skillet and sauté for about 5 to 10 minutes.
4. Add artichoke hearts and tarragon.
5. Make roux with butter and flour.
6. In saucepan, bring chicken broth to boil.
7. Add boiling chicken broth and sherry to roux, stirring with wire whisk to blend smoothly.
8. Pour over the chicken mixture.
9. Bake in a greased 9" x 13" casserole at 350° for 45 minutes.

❧ Serves 6 to 8

Is it not to deal thy bread to the hungry, and that thou bring the poor that are cast out to thy house? when thou seest the naked, that thou cover him; and that thou hide not thyself from thine own flesh?

—Isaiah 58:7

Stuffed Chicken

No longer do I have to flatten the chicken in this recipe. Just recently I have found thin chicken breasts available in our local grocery store. If you can't find them in yours and you want to save some time, ask your meat cutter at your grocer's to do the work for you while you do your shopping.

10 boneless chicken breast halves

10 slices deli ham

10 slices provolone cheese

½ cup flour

½ cup grated Parmesan cheese

1 teaspoon rubbed sage

¼ teaspoon paprika

Dash pepper

¼ cup vegetable oil

1 10.75-ounce can cream of celery soup

1 10.75-ounce can cream of chicken soup

1 cup chicken broth

1. Flatten chicken to ⅛" in thickness.
2. Place 1 slice of ham and 1 slice of cheese on each breast.
3. Roll up and tuck in ends and secure with a toothpick.
4. Mix together the flour, Parmesan cheese, sage, paprika, and pepper.
5. Dredge chicken in mixture.
6. Cover and refrigerate for 1 hour.
7. In a large skillet, brown chicken in oil over medium-high heat. Place in 9" × 13" baking dish when done.
8. Combine soups and broth and pour over chicken.
9. Bake in 9" × 13" baking dish at 325° for 30 to 45 minutes.

❧ Serves 10

I have shewed you all things, how that so labouring ye ought to support the weak, and to remember the words of the Lord Jesus, how he said, It is more blessed to give than to receive.

—*Acts 20:35*

Tex-Mex Chicken

If you would like this dish a little spicier, add some jalapeños to it and it will be sure to clean out your sinuses.

Cooking spray

1 14-ounce can fat-free chicken broth

1 4-ounce can drained chopped green chilies

1 cup chopped onion

1 cup fat-free sour cream

¾ teaspoon salt

½ teaspoon cumin

½ teaspoon freshly ground black pepper

2 10.5-ounce cans condensed 98% fat-free cream of chicken soup

1 clove minced garlic

20 to 24 6" corn tortillas

4 cups shredded cooked chicken breast

2 cups finely shredded Mexican blend cheese

1. Heat oven to 350°.
2. Coat a 9" × 13" baking dish with cooking spray.
3. In a large pan, combine broth, chilies, onion, sour cream, salt, cumin, pepper, soup, and garlic and mix well.
4. Bring to boil, stirring constantly.
5. Remove from heat.
6. Spread 1 cup mixture in dish.
7. Arrange 6 tortillas over soup mixture, breaking to fit dish.
8. Top with 1 cup chicken and ½ cup cheese.
9. Repeat layers, ending with the cheese.
10. Spread remaining soup mixture over cheese.
11. Bake 30 minutes or until bubbly.

❧ Serves 6 to 8

O give thanks unto the LORD; for he is good; for his mercy endureth for ever.

—1 Chronicles 16:34

Chicken à la Pineapple

Fruit and chicken just seem to go together. This version has a fruity teriyaki taste but isn't too sweet. You can purchase bottled teriyaki sauce and just add some sugar and pineapple to make this recipe even easier.

½ cup sugar

½ cup water

½ cup soy sauce

2 tablespoons oil

1 20-ounce can crushed pineapple

1 teaspoon ginger

½ teaspoon garlic powder

3 pounds boneless chicken

1. Combine ingredients, blending well.
2. Place chicken in greased 9" × 13" baking dish.
3. Cover and refrigerate for 4 hours, stirring occasionally.
4. Bake at 350° for 40 minutes.

Serves 8 to 10

Turkey with Cranberries

Looking for another way to use your leftover turkey from your holiday meals? Just eliminate the first four steps of this recipe and place the turkey over the cranberry sauce and heat for 10 to 15 minutes instead of 30.

¾ cup flour

¼ teaspoon pepper

8 boneless skinless turkey breast halves

¼ cup butter or margarine

1 cup fresh or frozen cranberries

1 cup water

½ cup packed brown sugar

1 tablespoon red wine vinegar

Dash ground nutmeg

1. In shallow bowl, combine flour and pepper.
2. Dredge the turkey in flour mixture.
3. In a large skillet, cook turkey in butter until browned on both sides.
4. Remove turkey and place in greased 9" × 13" baking dish.
5. In the same skillet, combine the cranberries, water, brown sugar, vinegar, and nutmeg.
6. Cover and simmer for 5 minutes.
7. Place sauce over turkey.
8. Bake at 350° for 30 minutes.

Serves 8 to 10

Creamy Turkey and Biscuits

This shortcut recipe gives comfort and says love to those who are the recipients of this old-fashioned cooking. These biscuits may not be quite as good as mom and grandma used to make, but all you have to do is open the can and place them on the top of this casserole.

^{1}/₃ cup chopped green pepper

^{1}/₃ cup chopped onion

3 tablespoons butter

1 10.75-ounce can cream of mushroom soup

1 soup can milk

1 cup cooked turkey, cubed

1 10-ounce package mixed vegetables, thawed

2 7.5-ounce tubes refrigerated buttermilk biscuits

^{3}/₄ cup shredded Cheddar cheese

1. In a large saucepan, sauté green pepper and onion in butter until tender.
2. Gradually add cream of mushroom soup and milk.
3. Stir until mixed well.
4. Bring to a boil.
5. Cook and stir for 2 minutes.
6. Stir in turkey and mixed vegetables.
7. Transfer to a greased 9" × 13" baking dish.
8. Separate biscuits and arrange over the top.
9. Sprinkle with the cheese.
10. Bake, uncovered, at 425° for 17 to 20 minutes or until golden brown.

Serves 8 to 10

Escalloped Chicken

Nostalgic recipes can instantly bring you back to your younger days. This is one such recipe. It reminds me of the times my parents and I used to go to the cafeteria in the union at Purdue University where one of their best dishes was escalloped chicken. The days of the cafeteria are over, but memories linger on.

1 rotisserie chicken purchased from store

4 tablespoons flour

4 tablespoons butter

1 quart chicken broth

^{1}/₄ teaspoon pepper

1 teaspoon salt

1^1/₂ quarts dry bread crumbs

2 beaten eggs

1 stalk celery, chopped

2 tablespoons onion, chopped

4 tablespoons butter or margarine, melted

1. Remove skin from chicken. Remove meat and cut into bite size pieces.
2. Place chicken meat in buttered 9" × 13" baking dish.
3. Melt butter over medium heat in skillet.
4. Add flour and stir until bubbly, gradually blending in broth with wire whisk.
5. Add pepper and salt and remove gravy from heat.

continued

(Escalloped Chicken—continued)

6. In medium bowl, combine bread crumbs, eggs, celery, onion, and butter.
7. Spoon bread crumb mixture over chicken.
8. Pour gravy over bread mixture.
9. Bake at 350° for 30 to 40 minutes.

❧ Serves 8 to 10

Behold, as wild asses in the desert, go they forth to their work; rising betimes for a prey: the wilderness yieldeth food for them and for their children.

—Job 24:5

Pam's Escalloped Chicken

Here's another escalloped chicken recipe, one that my old friend Pam gave me when our husbands were in the Navy. It's very easy, especially when you use the rotisserie chicken from your local grocery store.

1 large rotisserie chicken purchased from store
2½ cups croutons
Salt and pepper
1 pint whipping cream
1½ cups chicken broth

1. Remove chicken from bone. Place chicken in greased 9" × 13" baking dish.
2. Put croutons over chicken.
3. Add salt and pepper to taste.
4. Pour 1 pint whipping cream over chicken.
5. Pour chicken broth over whipping cream.
6. Bake at 325° for 40 to 50 minutes, then at 350° for 10 more minutes or until lightly browned.

❧ Serves 8 to 10

Crunchy Tuna

Everybody has their own favorite tuna recipes, and this is one of mine. I usually prefer to use the albacore tuna rather than the regular tuna, but it tastes good with either one.

½ cup chicken broth

1 10.75-ounce can cream of mushroom soup

1 10.75-ounce can cream of celery soup

3 cups diced cooked chicken

1 7-ounce can tuna, flaked

¼ cup minced onions

1 cup sliced celery

1 8-ounce can water chestnuts, thinly sliced

1 3-ounce can chow mein noodles

⅓ cup sliced almonds

1. Blend broth into soups in casserole.
2. Mix in remaining ingredients except almonds.
3. Bake at 325° for 45 to 50 minutes.
4. Sprinkle with almonds before serving.

❧ Serves 4

Country Captain Chicken Casserole

This is another recipe from Laura's family cookbook. (What a help Laura was in gathering recipes for this book!) The almonds and currants are a great addition to this recipe. Be sure to bring along a side of rice when you take this for a special occasion.

1 4-pound chicken cut in serving pieces, or 12 chicken breasts and thighs

Seasoned flour

½ cup shortening or oil

2 to 3 onions, finely chopped

1 to 2 green peppers, coarsely chopped

1 to 2 cloves garlic, minced

¼ to 4 teaspoons curry powder, according to taste

1½ teaspoons salt

Dash pepper

1 teaspoon thyme

2 20-ounce cans tomatoes

½ teaspoon to 1 tablespoon parsley, chopped

Hot cooked rice

¼ to 1 pound almonds, toasted

½ to ⅔ cup currants (optional)

Parsley sprigs

1. Skin chicken, dredge in flour, and fry in oil until brown.
2. Remove and keep warm.

continued

3. Cook onions, green peppers, garlic in remaining oil until tender.
4. Stir in curry powder, salt, pepper, thyme, tomatoes, and parsley.
5. Place chicken in large casserole or roaster pan and pour sauce over chicken.
6. Bake at 350° for 45 minutes or until tender.
7. Serve in a ring of rice or rice on the side.
8. Garnish chicken with almonds, currants, and parsley sprigs.

✺ Serves 8 to 10

Be not forgetful to entertain strangers:
for thereby some have entertained angels unawares.

—*Hebrews 13:2*

Chicken with White Barbecue Sauce

I was intrigued when my new friend Ellen told me about her recipe for chicken with white barbecue sauce. Since all of us love mayonnaise in our family, I thought we'd all like this recipe. I like it so well, I think I'll move in with Ellen for a while and partake of some of her good ol' southern cooking.

1 cup mayonnaise
2 tablespoons Worcestershire sauce
2 tablespoons vinegar
2 teaspoons ground black pepper
Vegetable cooking spray
8 to 10 chicken breasts

1. Combine all ingredients except chicken breasts in medium or large mixing bowl.
2. Blend well.
3. Spray 9" × 13" baking dish with vegetable cooking spray.
4. Place chicken in dish and pour marinade over it.
5. Marinate for 1 hour in refrigerator.
6. Preheat oven to 350° and bake chicken for 35 to 45 minutes.

✺ Serves 8 to 10

Fix-Ahead Chicken Casserole

Our longtime family friend Millie gave me this recipe to make the night before serving. I like to use fettuccine noodles in place of the elbow macaroni.

2 cups uncooked elbow macaroni

4 cups cooked diced chicken

1 10.75-ounce can cream of mushroom soup

1 10.75-ounce can cream of chicken soup

2 tablespoons onions

1 tablespoon chopped green pepper

8 ounces shredded American cheese, reserving part for top

1. Mix together all ingredients.
2. Place in a greased 9" × 13" baking dish.
3. Cover and refrigerate overnight.
4. Bake at 350° for 1 hour 30 minutes or until hot and bubbly.
5. At the last half hour of baking, sprinkle with reserved shredded cheese.

Serves 8 to 10

Ham and Cheesy Mashed Potatoes

Annis's friend Anna shared this recipe with her and she in turn shared it with me. It's wonderful that so many good cooks are willing to share their recipes and their cooking tips. As she has written in one of her loving poems, "Food brings people back to places they have been, family and friends need each other, time and time again."

8 cups mashed potatoes

1½ teaspoons garlic powder

3 cups diced fully cooked ham

3 cups shredded Cheddar cheese

1 cup whipping cream

1. In a large bowl, combine the mashed potatoes and garlic powder.
2. Put the potatoes into a greased 9" × 13" baking dish.
3. Distribute ham evenly over the potatoes.
4. Combine the cheese and the whipping cream.
5. Pour mixture over the ham.
6. Bake uncovered at 450° for 15 minutes or until golden.

Serves 12 to 15

Escalloped Cabbage

Ham and cabbage go hand in hand with each other. I was not familiar with this dish until I tried it at a church potluck dinner many years ago. Many a memory of stuffed cabbage dinners will come back when you serve this dish.

1 medium head cabbage, shredded

2 cups milk

2 tablespoons butter

3 tablespoons flour

2 cups cooked diced ham

1 cup bread crumbs

1 cup shredded cheese

1. Cook cabbage in boiling salted water for 3 to 5 minutes. Drain well.
2. In medium bowl, whisk together milk, butter, and flour.
3. Stir cabbage into sauce. Add ham
4. Place in greased 9" × 13" baking dish.
5. Cover with bread crumbs and cheese.
6. Bake at 350° for 30 to 35 minutes or until golden brown on top.

Serves 10 to 12

Pork Flautas

My friend Kathi discovered this recipe at a neighborhood cookout when she and her husband were stationed in Washington, D.C. She got this from another Air Force wife. You can get some of the best recipes from military wives!

Vegetable cooking spray

12 corn tortillas

10 ounces pork sausage

2 tablespoons chopped onion

1/3 cup shredded Cheddar cheese

2 ounces cream cheese, softened

1/4 teaspoon marjoram

1/3 cup sour cream

1. Soften tortillas by frying in a skillet sprayed with vegetable cooking spray.
2. Combine sausage, onion, cheese, cream cheese, and marjoram.
3. Place 2 tablespoons of filling in center of tortilla.
4. Roll up and bake at 375° for 35 minutes in a greased 9" × 13" baking dish.
5. Warm sour cream in microwave for 20 seconds and spoon over flautas.

Makes 12

Pork Chops and Rice

This recipe is so easy that your kids can put it together for you on a busy day. That's why Kathi liked it so well. Her kids would have it ready for her when she came home after a busy day taking care of patients.

1 10.75-ounce can cream of celery soup

1 10.75-ounce can cream of mushroom soup

2 cups rice, uncooked

1 cup milk

1 cup sour cream

8 pork chops

1. Mix together soups, rice, milk, and sour cream and pour into a greased 9" × 13" baking dish.
2. Place pork chops on top.
3. Cover and bake at 350° for 45 to 60 minutes until done.

 Serves 8

But Jesus said unto her, Let the children first be filled: for it is not meet to take the children's bread, and to cast it unto the dogs.

—Mark 7:27

April's Macaroni

My friend and neighbor April is always cooking up something good. She gave me a taste of this one night when I dropped by at supper time. She's a super neighbor and friend and always willing to share her recipes. This is an old recipe passed down from her great grandmother.

1 pound bacon

1 large onion

2 heels of bread, crumbled

1 46-ounce can tomato juice

1 16-ounce box elbow macaroni

1. Freeze bacon for an hour to make it easier to cut.
2. Cut up bacon into small pieces and dice onion.
3. Sauté bacon and onion in skillet until almost done.
4. Add bread and finish cooking until crisp and brown. Drain.
5. Cook macaroni as directed and drain.
6. Combine all ingredients including tomato juice and put in a 9" × 13" baking dish.
7. Bake at 350° for 30 minutes.
8. Serve with bread and butter.

 Serves 10 to 12

Barbecued Pulled Pork

Here's a Crock-Pot barbecue recipe that can cook all day and be ready at dinnertime with no hassles. Serve it on buns, with coleslaw either on the side or on your sandwich, my preference. April prefers Open Pit barbecue sauce, but you can use your favorite.

1 cup water
3 pounds boneless pork tenderloin, cut up
1 42-ounce bottle barbecue sauce
Buns
Cole slaw

1. Put water and cut-up pork tenderloin in Crock-Pot and cook for 8 to 10 hours or overnight, until it falls apart.
2. Drain and pull apart.
3. Add Open Pit barbecue sauce or your favorite barbecue sauce.
4. Cook an additional hour in Crock-Pot.

 Serves 12 to 14

Stuffed Zucchini

This recipe takes a little more time to make than most of the other recipes in this book, but it's worth it. It's a good way to use the zucchini that all your neighbors bring you in the summer from their gardens.

8 zucchinis, scrubbed, not peeled
3 tablespoons olive oil
1 cup finely chopped onions
½ teaspoon chopped jarred garlic
1 pound ground beef or Italian sausage or pork
2 eggs slightly beaten
1 cup Italian bread crumbs
1 cup Parmesan cheese
1 teaspoon oregano
1 teaspoon salt
½ teaspoon pepper
3 cups tomato sauce

1. Cut zucchini in half lengthwise and spoon out most of pulp, leaving boat-like shells. Set aside.
2. Chop pulp coarsely.
3. Heat 3 tablespoons of olive oil, add onions, and cook until soft and lightly colored.
4. Add pulp and garlic and cook 5 minutes longer. Transfer pulp mixture to bowl and set aside.
5. Brown meat in skillet, stirring constantly. When done, drain and add to pulp mixture in bowl.

continued

6. In another bowl, combine zucchini mixture and meat.
7. Beat eggs, bread crumbs, ½ cup of cheese, oregano, salt, and pepper into mixture.
8. Spoon into shells.
9. Pour tomato sauce in greased 9" × 13" baking dish.
10. Arrange zucchini on sauce.
11. Sprinkle with remaining cheese and cover with foil.
12. Bake at 350° for 20 to 30 minutes; remove foil and bake 10 minutes longer.

Serves 16

And they will salute thee, and give thee two loaves of bread; which thou shalt receive of their hands.

—1 Samuel 10:4

Broccoli and Ham Pasta

This is another good ham and cheese recipe. You can vary it by substituting another type of cheese and another type of pasta.

1 cup mayonnaise

2 10-ounce packages frozen broccoli florets, thawed and drained

2 cups shredded Swiss cheese

3 cups cooked ham, diced

2 cups rotini, cooked and drained

¾ cup chopped yellow pepper

½ cup milk

1 cup croutons

1. Combine mayonnaise, broccoli, 1½ cups cheese, ham, rotini, yellow pepper, and milk.
2. Put mixture into greased 9" × 13" baking dish.
3. Top with remaining cheese and croutons.
4. Bake at 350° for 30 minutes.

Serves 12

Chicken-Bacon Pizza

Easy to fix, easy to serve, easy to enjoy. Whip this up before a get-together and enjoy with your friends and loved ones.

4 ounces cream cheese, softened
½ cup sour cream
Vegetable cooking spray
1 8-ounce tube crescent rolls
½ cup bacon bits
1 10-ounce can chicken breast, drained
⅓ cup yellow peppers
⅓ cup green peppers
½ cup diced onions
½ cup sliced mushrooms
½ cup diced tomatoes

1. In a bowl, combine cream cheese and sour cream. Mix well.
2. Preheat oven to 375°.
3. Spray 9" pie pan with vegetable cooking spray.
4. Press crescent rolls into pie plate to form crust.
5. Spread cream cheese mixture evenly over crescent rolls.
6. Top cream cheese with bacon bits, chicken, and chopped vegetables.
7. Bake for 10 to 15 minutes. Cut into wedges and serve.

Serves 12

Mexican Lasagna

This is a different spin on lasagna that is quite a treat. You can make it spicier by adding some jalapeños to the cottage cheese mixture.

1 pound ground pork
½ cup chopped onion
½ cup chopped green pepper
2 cups diced tomato
1 1.25-ounce envelope taco seasoning
2 cups cottage cheese
2 eggs
6 flour tortillas
6 ounces shredded Cheddar cheese

Toppings:
½ cup diced tomatoes
¼ cup sliced olives
¼ cup sliced green onions

1. Brown ground pork with onion and pepper.
2. Add tomatoes and taco seasoning.
3. In a bowl, mix cottage cheese, Cheddar cheese, and eggs.
4. Grease a 9" × 13" baking dish and place 3 tortillas on bottom.
5. Spread tortillas with half of meat mixture and half of cottage cheese mixture.

continued

6. Layer with 3 tortillas and then remaining meat and cottage cheese mixture.
7. Bake uncovered at 350° for 40 minutes.
8. Remove from oven and add toppings.

❧ Serves 8 to 10

Greater love hath no man than this, that a man lay down his life for his friends.

—John 15:13

Biscuits and Gravy

This is comfort food at its best from Annis. I'm not sure I want to count the calories in this, but the flavor is wonderful. Savor every delicious bite.

1 pound sausage
1 10.75-ounce can cream of chicken soup
1 cup half-and-half
½ teaspoon dry mustard
¼ teaspoon seasoned salt
¼ teaspoon pepper
1 cup sour cream
1 7.5-ounce tube biscuits

1. In a heavy skillet, crumble sausage and cook over medium heat until browned.
2. Drain and remove sausage from skillet.
3. In the same skillet, mix soup and half-and-half.
4. Add mustard, salt, and pepper.
5. Bring to a boil.
6. Reduce heat and stir in sausage and sour cream.
7. Simmer until heated through but do not boil.
8. Split biscuits in half and place in greased 9" × 13" baking dish and pour gravy over biscuits.
9. Cover with foil to keep warm.

❧ Serves 10

Hash Brown Casserole

The French-fried onions give this recipe a nice crunchy taste. You may even want to double the amount of onions that are recommended.

1 8-ounce package cream cheese, softened
2 10.75-ounce cans cream of celery soup
1 32-ounce package frozen hash browns, thawed
1½ cups diced green peppers
2 cups cooked ham, cut into cubes
1 cup shredded Cheddar cheese
1 can French-fried onions

1. Cook cream cheese and soup in saucepan until blended, stirring with wire whisk.
2. Place hash browns in bowl and toss with soup mixture, peppers, and ham.
3. Put mixture in greased 9" × 13" baking dish.
4. Bake at 350° for 30 to 45 minutes.
5. Top with Cheddar cheese and French-fried onions and bake for 10 to 15 minutes more.

⊱ Serves 8 to 10

Stuffed Pork Casserole

This reminds me of a pork-and-dressing dish that Mom used to make. She always used pork chops and cut them off the bone before cooking. The boneless pork tenderloin makes this recipe a lot easier to prepare.

1 3-pound pork tenderloin, cut into ½" thick slices
2 10.75-ounce cans cream of chicken soup
1 14.5-ounce can chicken broth
¾ cup Miracle Whip
1 8-ounce canister of chicken-flavored Stove Top stuffing

1. Place pork in the bottom of a greased 9" × 13" baking dish.
2. Mix soup, broth, and Miracle Whip and heat in saucepan until warm.
3. Pour over pork.
4. Prepare stuffing mix by package directions.
5. Spoon stuffing evenly over chicken and soup mixture.
6. Bake at 350° for 45 minutes.

⊱ Serves 8 to 10

Pork Tenderloin and Potato Bake

This is one of Anita's recipes given to her by an old friend, Gladys. It's wonderful comfort food. Potatoes served with pork make for a hearty meal.

1 3-pound pork tenderloin, cut into ½" slices

1 10.75-ounce can cream of mushroom soup

½ cup milk

⅔ cup sour cream

2 cups shredded mild Cheddar cheese

½ teaspoon seasoned salt

1 32-ounce bag frozen plain hash brown potatoes, thawed

2 cans French-fried onions

1. Lightly brown each slice of tenderloin in 4 to 5 tablespoons oil.
2. Remove tenderloins onto platter.
3. Combine soup, milk, sour cream, 1 cup shredded cheese, and ½ teaspoon seasoned salt.
4. Pat thawed potatoes with paper towel to remove any water.
5. Stir soup mixture into thawed potatoes.
6. Spoon half of the potato mixture into greased 9" × 13" baking dish.
7. Arrange tenderloin pieces on top of potato mixture.
8. Spoon remaining potato mixture over tenderloin pieces.
9. Bake covered with foil for 30 minutes.
10. Sprinkle remaining shredded cheese over potatoes and top with onions.
11. Bake uncovered about 3 to 5 minutes longer or until cheese melts and onions are lightly browned.

❧ Serves 8 to 10

Man did eat angels' food:
he sent them meat to the full.

—Psalms 78:25

Stuffed Ham Rolls

Get deli ham sliced fairly thin. It tastes better than with the prepackaged ham. These would be good made with other deli meats such as turkey or chicken breast.

Nonstick cooking spray

1 cup chopped fresh spinach

1 cup cooked rice

2 green onions, sliced

¼ teaspoon pepper

1 pound deli ham slices

1 cup mayonnaise

2 tablespoons mustard

1. Spray 9" × 13" baking dish with nonstick cooking spray.
2. Wash and drain spinach. Pat dry with paper towel.
3. Combine rice, green onions, spinach, and pepper in a medium bowl.
4. Place 2 tablespoons rice mixture in the center of each ham slice.
5. Roll up and secure with toothpicks.
6. Lay the rolls in the bottom of the prepared pan.
7. Bake, covered, at 350° for 20 to 25 minutes until heated through.
8. Meanwhile, blend mayonnaise and mustard and warm in saucepan.
9. Top the ham rolls with the sauce and bake for 5 more minutes.

Makes 15 to 18 rolls

Smoked Pork Chop Casserole

This will satisfy all those meat and potato lovers at your next gathering. You can fix this the day before or in the morning early and then just pop it in the oven when you're ready to serve it. You won't have to worry about rushing or cleaning up the kitchen.

3 tablespoons margarine or butter

3 tablespoons flour

1 14.5-ounce can chicken broth

8 to 10 smoked pork chops

2 tablespoons oil

Salt and pepper

8 cups sliced potatoes

1 medium onion, sliced

1. In saucepan, melt margarine or butter.
2. Stir in flour, salt, and pepper.
3. Add chicken broth.
4. Cook and stir until mixture boils; boil for 2 more minutes.
5. Remove from heat and set aside.
6. In skillet, brown chops in oil with dash salt and pepper. Drain pork chops on paper towels.

continued

(Smoked Pork Chop Casserole—continued)

7. Place potatoes in greased 9" × 13" baking dish.
8. Top with onions.
9. Pour broth mixture over potatoes and onions.
10. Place pork chops on top and cover with aluminum foil. Bake at 350° for 50 to 60 minutes.
11. Uncover and bake 20 to 30 minutes more.

Serves 8 to 10

*He causeth the grass to grow for the cattle,
and herb for the service of man: that he may
bring forth food out of the earth.*

—Psalms 104:14

Shrimp Quiche

This is the only recipe I have from my niece Paula, who is a terrific cook. She also is the one who helped me get started writing cookbooks.

1 10" partially baked pie crust
Vegetable cooking spray
¼ cup finely chopped celery
1 small onion, thinly sliced
1 pound small frozen shrimp, thawed
1 cup shredded Swiss cheese
4 eggs, lightly beaten
2 cups cream
2 tablespoons parsley flakes
2 tablespoons sherry
¼ teaspoon nutmeg
½ teaspoon salt
¼ teaspoon pepper

1. Bake pie crust at 450° for 5 minutes.
2. Spray skillet with vegetable cooking spray and sauté celery and onion until just tender.
3. In large bowl, mix together remaining ingredients; add celery and onion and pour into baked pie shell.
4. Bake at 450° for 10 minutes.
5. Reduce heat to 350° and bake for another 10 to 15 minutes or until toothpick inserted comes out clean.

Serves 8

Shrimp Divan

You'll be making this recipe more often when the grocers offer shrimp on sale. The cooked and ready-to-eat shrimp makes it much easier to prepare seafood dishes. This would also be delicious with imitation crabmeat which I use often as it is less expensive to use and tastes great.

4 tablespoons butter

4 tablespoons flour

$2/3$ cup hot water

4 teaspoons chicken bouillon

$1/2$ cup whipping cream

4 tablespoons sherry

$1/4$ teaspoon nutmeg

$1/2$ cup shredded asiago cheese

20 ounces frozen broccoli spears, thawed

2 pounds cooked and ready-to-eat shrimp

4 tablespoons grated Parmesan cheese

Paprika

1. In medium saucepan, over medium heat, melt butter.
2. Blend in flour with wire whisk.
3. Stir in water, bouillon, cream, sherry, and nutmeg.
4. Cook until thickened, stirring often.
5. Stir in asiago cheese. Set aside.
6. Place broccoli in greased 9" × 13" baking dish.
7. Arrange shrimp on top.
8. Pour cream sauce over the broccoli.
9. Sprinkle with Parmesan and paprika.
10. Bake at 350° for 15 to 25 minutes.

Serves 8 to 10

Provideth her meat in the summer, and gathereth her food in the harvest.

—Proverbs 6:8

Chicken-Shrimp Rice Casserole

The combination of chicken and shrimp in this dish will satisfy both the chicken lover and the seafood lover. My sister Lois is very fond of this recipe since these are two of her favorite foods.

1 cup half-and-half

2 3-ounce containers cream cheese with chives, softened

2 tablespoons cornstarch

2½ cups chicken broth

4 cups cooked rice

4 cups cooked chicken breast

1 pound cooked ready-to-eat shrimp

¼ teaspoon paprika

1. Blend half-and-half gradually into cream cheese with electric beater and beat until smooth.
2. In saucepan, blend cornstarch and chicken broth and add cheese and half-and-half mixture.
3. Cook over medium heat until thick, stirring constantly.
4. Spread half the rice in the bottom of a greased 9" × 13" baking dish.
5. Place half the chicken and half the shrimp over the rice and pour half the sauce over this layer.
6. Repeat layers and sprinkle with paprika.
7. Bake at 350° for 30 minutes or until bubbly.

Serves 8 to 10

Shrimp-Crabmeat Seafood Casserole

I love to use the artificial crabmeat in my seafood casseroles as it is full of protein and good for you as well. Both shrimp and crabmeat are low in calories and provide you with a great taste.

1 6-ounce box long-grain and wild rice blend

2½ cups chicken broth

2 pounds artificial crabmeat

2 pounds cooked shrimp

1 14-ounce can artichokes, drained

1 10.75-ounce can cream of celery soup

½ cup mayonnaise

3 tablespoons onions, chopped

1 8-ounce can water chestnuts, drained and sliced

2 cups breadcrumbs

1. Cook the rice in the chicken broth according to the directions on the package.
2. Combine all ingredients and put them in a greased 9" × 13" baking dish.
3. Cover with foil. Bake at 350° for 45 minutes or until hot and bubbly.
4. Remove foil and brown.

Serves 8 to 10

Casserole for Seafood Lovers

Do you love seafood as much as I do? If so, here's a great and easy way to serve it for an entrée. Fix it for those seafood lovers that you know. I also like to substitute angel hair pasta for the macaroni, but any pasta that you like will work. You can break it up into pieces before adding it to the rest of the ingredients.

2 cups artificial crab flakes
2 cups cooked salad shrimp
1 cup evaporated milk or regular milk
3 cups chicken broth
1 cup uncooked pasta
¼ cup minced onion
2 cups shredded Swiss cheese
1 4-ounce can mushrooms drained
¼ teaspoon pepper
1 cup chopped celery
½ cup Parmesan cheese

1. Mix together all ingredients except Parmesan cheese and put in greased 9" × 13" baking dish.
2. Put Parmesan cheese on top.
3. Bake at 375° for 60 to 80 minutes.

❧ Serves 8 to 10

Shrimp and Mushroom Dumplings

For a satisfying supper dish, fix these dumplings along with salad and French bread, and you've got a great meal. The convenience items we can buy to make our cooking easier and our time spent cooking shorter are so plentiful and so available—take advantage of them.

Vegetable cooking spray
1 8-ounce can refrigerated crescent rolls
2 cups diced cooked shrimp
1 cup shredded three-cheese blend
1 8-ounce can mushroom stems and pieces, drained
1 10.75-ounce can cream of shrimp soup
½ cup milk

1. Coat 8" square baking dish with vegetable cooking spray.
2. Separate rolls.
3. Mix together shrimp, cheese, and mushrooms. Fill each roll with shrimp mixture.
4. Roll up starting at wide end.
5. Combine soup and milk and pour over rolls.
6. Bake at 400° for 20 to 25 minutes.

❧ Makes 8

Tuna and Pasta

Here's an economical dish that the whole family can enjoy. You can substitute broccoli or spinach for the frozen asparagus for a change. Also, try the tuna that now comes in a package instead of the can. You'll find it right with the rest of the tuna.

Vegetable cooking spray
1 cup chopped onion
1½ cups cooked small shell pasta
1 10.75-ounce can cream of celery soup
1 6-ounce can tuna, drained and flaked into pieces
½ cup sour cream
½ teaspoon dill weed
¼ cup milk
1 8-ounce package frozen asparagus spears, thawed

1. Preheat oven to 400°.
2. Coat skillet with vegetable cooking spray and sauté onion until tender.
3. Stir in pasta, soup, tuna, sour cream, dill, and milk. Mix well.
4. Cook 3 minutes or until hot.
5. Put asparagus into greased 2 quart baking dish.
6. Pour mixture over asparagus and bake for 15 minutes.

Serves 6

Crab-Mushroom Quiche

Gruyère cheese gives this quiche a wonderful creamy flavor. Look for this cheese in the deli section with the special cheeses. You can also substitute the Gruyère with one of your favorite cheeses. There are so many selections available in shredded cheeses and no dicing or cutting is required—nice!

1 4-ounce can sliced mushrooms
1 teaspoon butter
1 10" pastry shell, partially baked
1 16-ounce package artificial crab meat flakes
1⅓ cups finely diced Gruyère cheese
¾ cup sour cream
¼ cup mayonnaise
½ teaspoon salt
1 teaspoon flour
Light cream
3 eggs, slightly beaten
½ teaspoon hot pepper sauce

1. Drain mushrooms, reserving liquid.
2. Sauté mushrooms in butter for 2 minutes.
3. Scatter mushrooms in partially baked pie shell.
4. Place crab meat over mushrooms.
5. In a bowl, mix Gruyère cheese, sour cream, and mayonnaise with reserved mushroom liquid, salt, and flour.

continued

Hurry Curry

6. Add enough light cream to mixture to make 2 cups.
7. Blend in eggs and hot pepper sauce and pour into shell.
8. Bake at 350° for 55 minutes or until set.
9. Let stand 15 minutes before cutting.

❧ Serves 6 to 8

And thou shalt have goats' milk enough
for thy food, for the food of thy household,
and for the maintenance for thy maidens.

—Proverbs 27:27

I used to make this recipe before my husband became allergic to shrimp. Now I make it with cream of chicken soup and cooked chicken instead of the shrimp ingredients. I still serve it with my favorite chutney, Major Grey's. If you can't find this chutney in your grocery store, be sure to ask them if they carry it. It's not always with the condiments and can be hard to find.

½ teaspoon curry powder
½ cup chopped onion
1 tablespoon butter
1 10.75-ounce can cream of shrimp soup
1 cup sour cream
1 cup cooked shrimp
2 cups cooked rice
Chutney

1. Sauté curry powder and onion, in butter. Add soup to mixture.
2. Add sour cream and shrimp to soup mixture. Pour into greased 8" × 8" square baking dish.
3. Bake at 350° for 10 minutes.
4. Serve over rice.
5. Serve with chutney. Raisins, currants, scallions, and peanuts are some other tasty offerings to serve with curry.

❧ Serves 4 to 6

June's Salmon Loaf

My dear friend June, who turned 80 years young this year, shared this delicious salmon recipe with me. June appears and looks at least 10 years younger than her chronological age. She is a special friend and one amazing woman.

1 cup cooked instant rice

¾ cup cracker crumbs

2 eggs

½ teaspoon salt

1 tablespoon chopped onion

2 cans flaked canned salmon

2 teaspoons lemon juice

1. Combine all ingredients in medium bowl.
2. Place in a buttered 9" × 5" × 3" loaf pan.
3. Bake at 350° for 30 to 40 minutes.

Serves 6 to 8

Tortellini and Garlic Cream Sauce

For those of you who are not fond of shrimp, this recipe would taste just as good with chicken. You can also substitute half-and-half for the heavy cream in this recipe to cut down on the calories. One of my dear friends, Sharnell, shared this recipe with me. What would we do without good friends!

1 19-ounce package frozen tortellini

1 tablespoon olive oil

6 tablespoons butter

2 teaspoons minced jarred garlic

2 pounds frozen cooked shrimp, thawed

½ cup heavy cream

1 teaspoon salt and pepper to taste

2 teaspoons Italian seasoning blend

2 tablespoons parsley

1. Prepare tortellini according to package directions.
2. Cook same time as sauce. When finished, toss with olive oil and set aside.
3. In medium skillet, melt butter and sauté garlic on medium heat for 3 to 5 minutes.
4. Add shrimp and sauté for 3 to 5 more minutes.
5. Add cream, salt, pepper, and Italian seasoning blend.
6. Bring to a simmer.
7. Toss sauce, pasta, and parsley in large bowl.
8. Cover with foil to keep warm.

Serves 10

Tuna-Cashew Casserole

Cashews and chow mein noodles give this tuna casserole an extra crunch. We used to have this at home on Fridays when we couldn't eat any meat. It became quite a staple in our house.

2 10.75-ounce cans cream of mushroom soup

½ cup water

2 6-ounce cans tuna

1 cup cashew pieces

2 cups diced celery

½ cup finely diced green peppers

½ cup shredded Cheddar cheese

4 chopped pimientos

1 cup chow mein noodles

1. Combine all ingredients except noodles and put in buttered 9" × 13" pan.
2. Top with noodles.
3. Bake at 325° for 40 minutes.

Serves 12

Seafood Tetrazzini

I haven't seen my cousin Susie for quite some time. She and her sister Barb were always our city cousins from Chicago, and we were always the small-town girls from Indiana. This recipe of hers will delight everyone, no matter where they dwell.

2 tablespoons chopped onion

1 tablespoon butter

1 10.75-ounce can cream of mushroom soup

1 cup half-and-half

2 tablespoons dry sherry

8 ounces thin spaghetti, cooked

3 cups cooked shrimp

¼ cup chopped green peppers

¾ pound mushrooms

2 tablespoons chopped pimiento

½ cup grated Parmesan cheese

1. Cook onion in butter until tender.
2. Blend in soup, half-and-half, and sherry with onion. Do not boil.
3. Add spaghetti, shrimp, peppers, mushrooms, and pimiento to soup mixture.
4. Pour into a greased 2-quart casserole and sprinkle with Parmesan cheese.
5. Bake covered at 375° for 30 minutes.
6. If dry, add more half-and-half or sherry.

Serves 4 to 6

Shrimp Casserole

I just saw my cousin Barbara recently when she came to Indiana to visit my sisters, Anita and Lois. I drove over, and what a great time we had, laughing and crying over all the good times we had shared. She gave me this recipe along with several others for everyone to enjoy.

3 cups cooked shrimp

2 hard-cooked eggs, chopped

1 4-ounce can sliced mushrooms

½ cup slivered almonds

¾ cup diced celery

1 tablespoon chopped onion

1 10.75-ounce can cream of chicken soup

¾ cup mayonnaise

1 5-ounce can chow mein noodles

1. Combine all ingredients except noodles in greased 2-quart casserole.
2. Sprinkle noodles on top.
3. Bake at 350° for 30 minutes.

Serves 4 to 6

Crustless Quiche

Kathi's daughter Jenny and her father used to make this every Sunday after church. Kathi can still see Jenny sitting on a little stool giving her dad the directions for the recipe. Kathi and her son Bryan had to clean up the mess that Bill and Jenny made.

1 stick butter or margarine

½ cup flour

6 large eggs

1 cup milk

16 ounces Monterey jack cheese, cubed

1 3-ounce package cream cheese, softened

2 cups cottage cheese

½ teaspoon salt

1 teaspoon sugar

1 teaspoon baking powder

1 pound frozen cooked shrimp, thawed

1. Melt butter and stir in flour with whisk.
2. Beat eggs and milk and add to flour mixture.
3. Add in cheeses and mix with wire whisk.
4. Add salt, sugar, baking powder, and shrimp.
5. Pour into greased 9" × 13" baking dish.
6. Bake at 350° for 45 minutes.

Serves 8 to 10

Crab Casserole

This recipe is similar to one my neighbor MaryAnn makes. I make it for brunches and for dinner, and everyone seems to love it at any time of day.

Vegetable cooking spray
½ cup chopped celery
½ cup chopped onion
1 cup diced green pepper
12 slices white bread
1 16-ounce package artificial crab flakes
½ cup salad dressing
4 eggs
3 cups milk
1 10.75-ounce can cream of mushroom soup
1 cup shredded asiago cheese

1. In skillet sprayed with vegetable cooking spray, sauté celery, onion, and pepper for 3 to 5 minutes until barely tender.
2. Break bread into pieces and put in greased 9" × 13" baking dish.
3. Combine crab, sautéed vegetables, and salad dressing and spoon over bread crumbs.
4. Combine eggs and milk and pour over all.
5. Bake at 350° for 15 minutes.
6. Spoon soup over top and scatter cheese over soup.
7. Bake at 325° for 45 to 60 minutes.
8. Let stand for a few minutes before serving.

🍤 Serves 8 to 10

Pasta with Crab and Feta Cheese

This is one of Gayle's favorite pasta recipes, which she recently shared with me. The feta cheese gives this a really creamy flavor. You may substitute any other kind of cheese you like for the feta.

2 teaspoons jarred minced garlic
4 tablespoons olive oil, divided
1 16-ounce package artificial crab flakes
1 12-ounce jar roasted red peppers, drained and finely chopped
16 ounces farfalle bow-tie pasta
4 4-ounce packages feta cheese with basil and tomato
1 tablespoon parsley

1. Cook and stir garlic in 2 tablespoons of the olive oil on medium heat for 3 minutes.
2. Add crab meat, red peppers, and remaining 2 tablespoons olive oil.
3. Cook 2 minutes or until thoroughly heated.
4. Cook pasta as directed on package. Drain.
5. Toss crab mixture with hot pasta and feta cheese.
6. Sprinkle with parsley.
7. When carrying this to an event, put in 9" × 13" buttered baking dish and cover with foil to keep warm.

🍤 Serves 8 to 10

$\mathcal{P}$otpourri

Wedding Disaster

My sister Marilyn and her husband Paul celebrated their 50th wedding anniversary in December 2004. What an accomplishment, especially when I think back to the day they were married. After the ceremony, at St. Boniface in Lafayette, Indiana, everyone came to our house for the wedding reception. Talk about good food! Marilyn, who was wearing our sister Lois's wedding dress and veil, was glowing—happiness was in the air. She came into the kitchen where all the food was being prepared to find Mom. Without realizing it, she got too close to our gas stove—the burners, of course, were on. As she turned around, my cousin Shirley was the first to see that her veil had caught fire. She quickly grabbed the crown of the veil off Marilyn's head, threw it in the sink, and ran water over it. Shirley's fast thinking saved my sister. Marilyn's eyebrows were singed, and of course she was in shock for a few minutes. Mother, of course, was a nervous wreck just thinking about what could have happened to one of her precious girls, but Dad calmed all of his girls down and the gaiety soon resumed.

What a day to remember. And fifty years later, we can still remember it as if it had happened yesterday. I can't really remember the food we had, but I know it was good, as it always was at our house. Thanks to Kodak, I can remember the cake—it was from our favorite bakery, O'Rears, which I still visit when I go back to Lafayette.

Poppy Seed Dressing

Kathi has kept this recipe for twenty years since receiving it from her golf buddy Pearl. If you would like to make it sugar-free and lower the calories, try using sugar substitute in place of the sugar and applesauce in place of the oil. I can't believe Kathi and I have been great friends for twenty years. Friends are such a blessing!

1½ cups sugar

2 teaspoons dry mustard

1 teaspoon salt

½ cup vinegar

1 tablespoon grated onion

2 cups oil

2 tablespoons poppy seeds

1. Blend together sugar, mustard, salt, and vinegar.
2. Add onion and oil. Beat until thick.
3. Add poppy seeds.
4. Refrigerate and serve.

❧ Makes 1 quart

Cranberry Crunch

Make this cranberry crunch especially around the holiday season. It seems that holidays and cranberries are synonymous. My friend Annis tells me this is good served with ice cream and/or whipped topping. She has shared many of her recipes from her collection for all of us to enjoy.

1 16-ounce can whole cranberry sauce

½ cup quick-cooking oats

½ cup packed brown sugar

¼ cup flour

4 tablespoons butter

Frozen whipped topping, thawed

1. Preheat oven to 350°.
2. Spread cranberry sauce in the bottom of a 9" pie pan.
3. In a small bowl, combine oats, brown sugar, and flour.
4. Cut in the butter until mixture is crumbly.
5. Sprinkle mixture over cranberry sauce.
6. Bake at 350° for 25 minutes.
7. When serving, top with whipped topping.

❧ Makes 3 cups

Cinnamon Pecans

You'll want to at least double this recipe so you'll have enough to share. They make great little gifts during the holiday season. Put them in a holiday tin and wish your family and friends happy holidays with these treats.

2½ cups pecan halves
2 tablespoons oil
1 cup sugar
1 teaspoon cinnamon
¼ teaspoon salt
¼ cup water
1 teaspoon vanilla

1. Toss pecans with oil.
2. Bake on a flat cookie sheet at 325° for 15 minutes. Stir often.
3. In a small saucepan, mix sugar, cinnamon, salt, water, and vanilla.
4. Cook until at a soft boil, about 3 to 5 minutes.
5. Mix with nuts and spread quickly on wax paper.
6. When cool, break apart into pieces.

🐸 Makes 3 cups

Crab Louis Dressing

I've used this recipe since I received it from one of my Navy friends when we were stationed in San Francisco. Crab Louis was a very popular dish in California, and we always loved it, so I learned to make this wonderful salad at home using this dressing.

1 cup mayonnaise
¼ cup heavy cream, whipped
¼ cup chili sauce
¼ cup chopped green pepper
¼ cup chopped green onion
1 teaspoon lemon juice
Salt

1. Mix together mayonnaise, whipped cream, chili sauce, green pepper, and green onion.
2. Add lemon juice.
3. Salt to taste.
4. Chill.

🐸 Makes 2 cups

Lois's Best Dressing

I love to keep this dressing in my refrigerator so I have it on hand for my salads. This is one of the best home-made dressings I've ever had, and it's become a real favorite in our family.

1½ cups light brown sugar
½ teaspoon paprika
½ cup ketchup
½ teaspoon salt
1 teaspoon onion powder
1½ cups vegetable oil
½ cup vinegar
½ teaspoon celery seed
½ teaspoon garlic

1. Mix sugar, paprika, ketchup, salt, and onion powder.
2. Add oil and vinegar alternately.
3. Add celery seed and garlic.
4. Keep refrigerated.

❧ Makes 1 quart

Hot Fudge Sauce

Just heat this up in the microwave when you're in the mood for a hot fudge sundae. Usually when I make it, I double the recipe so it will last for a longer period of time. Who doesn't love chocolate!

1 13-ounce can of evaporated milk
½ cup margarine
4 tablespoons unsweetened cocoa
4 tablespoons flour
2 cups sugar
2 teaspoons vanilla

1. In saucepan, combine milk and margarine and cook over medium heat until margarine melts.
2. Slowly stir in cocoa, flour, and sugar, stirring constantly.
3. While stirring, boil for a few minutes.
4. Stir in 2 teaspoons of vanilla.
5. Remove from heat and store in refrigerator when cool.

❧ Makes 2 cups

Hot Spiced Cider

Take this to your neighbors on a cold winter day or invite your neighbor over to share a cup while you sit around the fireplace and relax. My granddaughter's teacher just introduced her and her classmates to this soothing drink and now she has learned to make it.

1 tablespoon whole cloves

3 cinnamon sticks

2 quarts apple cider

¼ unpeeled lemon, thinly sliced

⅓ cup sugar

1. Place cloves and cinnamon sticks in a cheese-cloth bag and tie with string.
2. Place cider, lemon slices, sugar, and bag of spices in large pan and heat thoroughly.
3. Remove bag of spices.
4. Serve hot.

❧ Makes 16 cups

For the bread of God is he which cometh down from heaven, and giveth life unto the world.

—John 6:33

Pecan Treats

Didn't we all love the pie crust scraps Mom had left over when she made pies? This recipe reminds me of Mom and how we put cinnamon sugar on the pie crust pieces and baked them. There are never any of these left to bring home from potluck or picnics.

1 refrigerated pie crust, at room temperature for 5 to 10 minutes

1½ sticks butter or margarine

1 cup sugar

1 teaspoon cinnamon

1½ cups pecan pieces

½ teaspoon vanilla flavoring or extract

1. Unfold pie crust and place in greased pizza pan.
2. Punch holes with fork in pie crust.
3. In medium saucepan, combine butter, sugar, and cinnamon and cook over medium heat until mixture comes to a boil.
4. Boil for 1½ minutes.
5. Remove from heat, add pecans and vanilla, and stir.
6. Pour mixture over pie crust, spreading evenly.
7. Bake at 375° for 15 to 20 minutes or until golden.
8. When cool, break into pieces.

❧ Makes 20 to 24

Miniature Fruitcakes

I'm not big on fruitcake, but these moist mini ones Lois makes are delicious!

1 pound dates, pitted, already chopped
1 pound candied pineapple, cut into small pieces
1 pound candied cherries, cut into small pieces
1 pound chopped English walnuts
2½ cups sifted flour
2 teaspoons baking powder
8 eggs
1 teaspoon salt
1½ cups sugar
3 teaspoons vanilla
Vegetable cooking spray
Apple jelly, heated

1. Prepare fruit and nuts in large bowl.
2. Combine flour and baking powder. Sift over fruit and nuts and stir until all clings together.
3. Beat together eggs, salt, sugar, and vanilla.
4. Add to the fruit mixture and combine well.
5. Pack into 1¾" muffin pans sprayed with vegetable cooking spray.
6. Bake at 275° for 40 minutes. Put a 9" × 13" baking dish of hot water on bottom rack of oven while baking. This will help to keep the fruitcakes moist.
7. Remove with a serrated knife.
8. Brush with heated apple jelly for glaze.

Makes 24

Spiced Pecans

Try this recipe using walnuts for a change. They're a little cheaper to use but still have a great taste. You can freeze them or store them in a tight container. I make a few batches at one time and freeze them so I'll have some special snacks ready for any occasion.

1 egg white
1 tablespoon water
½ cup sugar
½ teaspoon allspice
½ teaspoon cinnamon
½ teaspoon salt
½ pound pecans

1. Beat egg white and water with whisk until foamy but not stiff.
2. In a large bowl, mix together sugar, allspice, cinnamon, and salt.
3. Put nuts in egg white and stir to coat thoroughly.
4. Remove them with a slotted spoon and toss well in the sugar mixture.
5. Bake on a greased cookie sheet at 275° for 1 hour, stirring the nuts every 15 minutes.

Makes ½ pound

Chex Mix

Christmas isn't Christmas without Chex Mix, and I think that applies to everybody's family. This one my sister Lois makes is my favorite combination. It might become yours, too. It's an addictive combination of sweet and salty—it's hard to stop eating it once you start.

1 cup Wheat Chex
1 cup Corn Chex
1 cup Rice Chex
1 cup Honey Nut Cheerios
1 cup Golden Grahams
1 cup pretzels
1 cup nuts
1 cup bagel chips
1 cup rye chips
¼ pound butter
½ tablespoon Worcestershire sauce
½ tablespoon garlic juice

1. Put all ingredients in large bowl except butter, Worcestershire sauce, and garlic juice.
2. Melt butter and add Worcestershire sauce and garlic juice.
3. Pour over cereal and pretzel mixture.
4. Bake in oven at 200° for 1 hour, stirring every 15 minutes.

Makes 10 cups

Chinese Fried Walnuts

These walnuts make great snacks any time of the year. Be sure to follow the directions carefully and separate them with a fork when removing them from the hot oil. These are hard to resist, but a great addition to a candy or snack tray.

6 cups boiling water
4 cups walnuts
½ cup sugar
Vegetable oil
¼ teaspoon salt

1. Cook walnuts in boiling water for 1 minute.
2. Drain and rinse walnuts with cold water.
3. Put on paper towels and dry well.
4. In medium bowl, combine sugar with walnuts.
5. In large skillet, fill with vegetable oil to about 1 inch deep. Deep-fry sugar-coated walnuts at 350° for 3 to 5 minutes.
6. Drain on wax paper and sprinkle lightly with salt.

Makes 4 cups

For we being many are one bread, and one body: for we are all partakers of that one bread.

—*1 Corinthians 10:17*

Salads

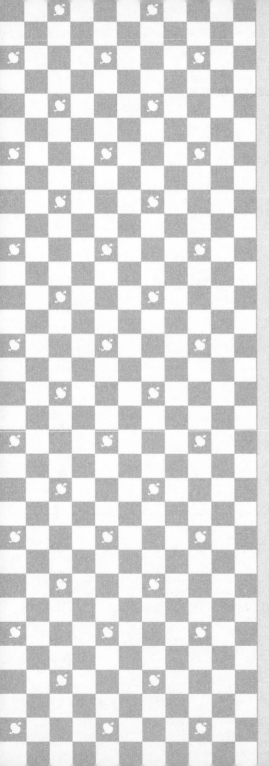

Navy Wife

*P*otlucks and carry-ins bring back many warm and funny memories. One of my first carry-in experiences was particularly memorable. It happened when my husband Larry was an admiral's aide back in the late '60s. His assignment was in Oakland, California, and we lived on the naval base, Treasure Island, located in between San Francisco and Oakland, in the San Francisco Bay. Every day we had a breathtaking view of San Francisco from our living room window.

Two weeks after we arrived, the admiral's wife asked me to attend a carry-in luncheon for new Navy wives in the area. Since we were not yet settled, I decided to make it easy on myself and bring a seven-layer salad. The morning of the luncheon, I woke up early and quickly put it together. I dropped my son off at the base nursery and arrived at the admiral's home five minutes late—fashionably late, as they used to say. I walked up the steps carefully with a tight grip on my salad. I'm very accident prone, so I was trying to be cautious.

As I rang the doorbell, I became a little jittery, wanting to make sure that I did and said the right thing. The admiral's wife greeted me with a warm smile and friendly manner. As I stepped into the house, her big black Lab came running up to me. I still don't know quite how it all happened, but the next thing I knew, the salad was all over the floor, all over the dog, and all over me. I could have died of humiliation! She couldn't have been more gracious. After everything was all cleaned up, including the dog and me, she joked with me about my "tossed" salad. I can't remember how many times I apologized. As you can see, I have never forgotten my first carry-in, and I will fondly remember the kindness and warm hospitality I received. ∾

Macaroni Salad

What's a picnic without macaroni salad? This version uses sweetened condensed milk, and it is out of this world. Make it for your next summer picnic. Thanks again, Annis.

2 16-ounce packages macaroni
1 cup chopped green pepper
½ cup chopped onion
1 cup chopped celery
1 cup shredded carrots
1 cup chopped yellow pepper
1 14-ounce can sweetened condensed milk
1 cup vinegar
1 cup sugar
2 cups mayonnaise
¼ teaspoon salt
¼ teaspoon pepper

1. Prepare the macaroni according to package directions.
2. Drain when finished and let cool in a large bowl.
3. When cool, add all the vegetables to the macaroni.
4. In a small bowl, using a whisk, combine the condensed milk and remaining ingredients.
5. After making the dressing, pour it over the macaroni and vegetables and toss together, coating mixture evenly.
6. Refrigerate a few hours before serving.

Serves 14 to 16

My Favorite Seven-Layer Salad

Everyone seems to have his or her own version of this very popular salad. Easy to prepare, great tasting—no wonder it is a staple at a lot of church dinners.

1 head of lettuce, torn into pieces
1 cup spinach leaves
1 cup chopped onion
1 cup chopped yellow peppers
1 can sliced water chestnuts, drained
1 10-ounce package of frozen asparagus spears, thawed
½ pound shredded deli ham
2 cups finely shredded Cheddar and Monterey jack cheeses
2 cups light mayonnaise
¼ cup sugar

1. In 9" × 13" dish, cover the bottom of the pan with the lettuce and spinach.
2. Layer onion, peppers, water chestnuts, asparagus, ham, and cheese in that order.
3. In a small bowl, combine mayonnaise and sugar and stir until smooth.
4. With a spatula, spread the mayonnaise and sugar mixture over salad.
5. Refrigerate until ready to serve.

Serves 12

Chinese Chicken Salad

There are many versions of this recipe, and I like them all. But then there aren't too many foods that I don't like. As with many other favorite recipes, I first tasted this at a carry-in at my husband's office.

1 head Napa cabbage, shredded
½ cup shredded carrots
¾ cup sliced green onions
1 8-ounce can sliced water chestnuts, drained
12 ounces cooked chicken breasts, shredded
¾ cup slivered almonds, toasted

Dressing:
1 cup vegetable oil
4 tablespoons rice vinegar
4 tablespoons soy sauce
2 teaspoons chicken bouillon
2 teaspoons sugar substitute
4 teaspoons toasted sesame seeds

1. In large bowl, toss together the cabbage, carrots, green onions, and water chestnuts.
2. Top with chicken and almonds and refrigerate.
3. In a small bowl, combine all ingredients for the dressing and refrigerate. When time to serve, pour on desired amount of dressing and toss together.

Serves 6 to 8

Corned Beef Salad

I received this recipe when I was in the PTO—Parent Teacher Organization—with another volunteer, Louise. She and I especially like to make it during the summer months. It's more than a salad since it has vegetables and beef in it.

1 3-ounce package lemon gelatin
1 cup boiling water
2 tablespoons vinegar
1 12-ounce can corned beef
2 cups chopped celery
½ cup chopped onion
3 hard-boiled eggs, chopped
1 10-ounce package frozen peas, cooked and drained
1¾ cups mayonnaise
¼ cup ketchup

1. Dissolve lemon gelatin in boiling water.
2. Add vinegar, corned beef, celery, onion, hard-boiled eggs, peas, and 1 cup of mayonnaise.
3. Put in greased 9" × 13" dish and refrigerate until set.
4. When set, spread with remaining ¾ cup mayonnaise mixed with the ketchup.

Serves 12

Hot Turkey Salad

Here's another great way to use your leftover turkey from Thanksgiving. It also tastes great with chicken or ham. The shredded Cheddar and Monterey jack cheese combination is only one of the many varieties you'll find available at your grocer's. Two of my other favorites are the four cheeses and the Italian cheeses. Thanks to Annis's friend Lou.

4 cups chopped cooked turkey

2 cups finely chopped celery

2 cups mayonnaise

½ cup chopped almonds, toasted

½ cup chopped onion

2 cups cooked rice

1 cup shredded Cheddar and Monterey jack cheeses

1 cup crushed potato chips

1. Combine turkey, celery, mayonnaise, almonds, and onion in a large mixing bowl.
2. Mix with rice.
3. Spoon into a greased 9" × 13" baking dish, cover, and bake at 350° for 15 minutes.
4. Sprinkle cheese and potato chips on top and return to oven for 5 to 10 minutes.

Serves 8 to 10

Pasta Salad

It's easy to make or my sister Lois wouldn't be making it. If she cooks at all, Lois always wants something that's quick to fix and tastes great. She makes this for her son Joe, as it is one of his favorites.

4 cups tricolor rotini, uncooked

Sugar substitute or sugar to taste

¾ cup Kraft Three-Cheese Italian dressing

1 3-ounce can sliced black olives, drained

1 10-ounce can chicken breast, drained

1. Cook rotini as directed on package.
2. Drain.
3. Mix together dressing and sugar substitute.
4. Toss rotini with dressing.
5. Add olives and chicken, tossing together lightly.
6. Refrigerate until time to serve.

Serves 8 to 10

Strawberry Salad

Here's another family holiday favorite, but you can make this any time of the year. Frozen strawberries will have some juice, but if you use fresh strawberries, mash a few of them to make some juice and add to your strawberries.

2 3-ounce packages strawberry gelatin

1½ cups boiling water

2 10-ounce packages frozen strawberries, partially thawed

1 13-ounce can crushed pineapple, undrained

1 8-ounce package cream cheese, softened

½ cup sour cream

1. Dissolve gelatin in boiling water.
2. Stir in strawberries and add pineapple.
3. Pour half of mixture into 9" × 13" baking dish.
4. Refrigerate until set.
5. Keep remaining mixture at room temperature.
6. Beat cream cheese until soft, add sour cream, and beat until smooth.
7. Spread cream cheese mixture over gelatin in dish. Refrigerate for 10 minutes. Add remaining gelatin mixture.

Serves 12 to 15

Sauerkraut Salad

This 75-year-old recipe was given to Lois by my Aunt Ceil. Sauerkraut was a favorite in their family since they came over from Germany in the early 1900s. I always add a little bit more sugar to it.

1 32-ounce can sauerkraut, drained and rinsed

1 cup finely chopped green or red peppers

½ cup finely chopped celery

½ cup finely chopped onion

1 cup sugar

½ cup diced radishes

½ cup shredded carrots

1. Combine all ingredients in medium bowl.
2. Cover bowl and refrigerate overnight.

Serves 12 to 15

And as they did eat, Jesus took bread, and blessed, and brake it, and gave to them, and said, Take, eat: this is my body.

—Mark 14:22

Tasty Slaw

It's a lot easier to make slaw now that you can buy the prepackaged cole slaw mix that is available in your local grocery store produce department. This is a classic dish with a special twist.

½ cup vinegar

2 tablespoons flour

¼ cup sugar

1 tablespoon prepared mustard

1 tablespoon celery seed

1 16-ounce package coleslaw

½ cup chopped Vidalia onions

½ cup chopped green peppers

1. In skillet, blend together vinegar, flour, sugar, mustard, and celery seed over medium heat.
2. Add vegetables and stir until mixture is thickened and add vegetables.
3. Remove from heat.
4. Serve warm or cold.

Serves 8 to 10

Layered Potato Salad

This is a different take on the classic potato salad that we all love. My friend Linda shared Eureatha's recipe with me for this book, as it has been at many a church potluck. Try it for your next one.

First Layer:

1 12-ounce can corned beef, chopped

¼ cup chili sauce

1 tablespoon finely chopped onion

2 teaspoons prepared mustard

1 teaspoon horseradish

1 envelope unflavored gelatin, divided in half

¼ cup water

½ cup mayonnaise

Second Layer:

2½ cups cooked, diced potatoes

½ cup diced celery

2 tablespoons finely chopped onions

1 teaspoon salt

Dash pepper

2 tablespoons finely chopped green pepper

¼ cup water

½ cup mayonnaise

2 teaspoons vinegar

continued

Another Oriental Salad

1. Combine corned beef, chili sauce, onion, mustard, and horseradish.
2. Soften half package of gelatin in ¼ cup hot water until dissolved; stir into ½ cup mayonnaise and add to the beef mixture.
3. Spread and press into greased 9" × 13" dish and chill until firm.
4. In a large bowl, combine potatoes, celery, onions, salt, pepper, and green peppers.
5. Dissolve the other half package of gelatin in ¼ cup hot water.
6. Blend in mayonnaise and vinegar.
7. Mix well and pour over potato mixture.
8. Toss potato mixture until well coated and spoon on top of corned beef mixture.
9. Chill until firm.

Serves 12 to 15

I went down into the garden of nuts to see the fruits of the valley, and to see whether the vine flourished and the pomegranates budded.

—Song of Solomon 6:11

With so many oriental salad recipes out there, it's hard to choose one. I've included three in this section of my book. Try all three and pick your favorite.

1 head Napa cabbage, shredded

1 bunch sliced green onions

2 3-ounce packages ramen noodles

Vegetable cooking spray

4 ounces slivered almonds

½ cup sesame seeds

1 cup oil

1 cup sugar

2 tablespoons soy sauce

½ cup vinegar

1. Combine cabbage and green onions in large bowl and set aside.
2. Crumble ramen noodles (this can be done while still in package).
3. Spray skillet with vegetable cooking spray.
4. Sauté the almonds, sesame seeds, and Ramen noodles in the skillet.
5. In a small bowl, combine the oil, sugar, soy sauce, and vinegar.
6. Mix well.
7. Combine all ingredients when serving.

Serves 6 to 8

Veggie Salad

This is bound to become a regular on your summer menu. You can use fresh vegetables instead of frozen during the summer. Try a combo of cauliflower, broccoli, zucchini, and yellow squash.

Salad:
1 16-ounce package frozen mixed vegetables, cooked until crisp and drained
½ cup chopped onions
1 cup chopped celery
½ cup chopped green pepper
½ cup chopped yellow pepper
1 15-ounce can red beans, drained

Dressing:
¾ cup sugar
½ cup vinegar
1 tablespoon mustard
2 tablespoons flour
¼ teaspoon salt

1. Place dressing ingredients in medium saucepan and cook until thick.
2. Remove from heat and cool.
3. Stir into vegetables and refrigerate until time to serve.

Serves 6 to 8

Tuna Salad

I had to try this recipe since it is a very strange combination of soup, gelatin, and tuna fish. It's much better than it sounds—in fact, it's delicious. I like to fix it in the summer for get-togethers.

1 3-ounce package of lemon gelatin
1 teaspoon unflavored gelatin
½ cup boiling water
1 10.75-ounce can chicken noodle soup
1 6-ounce can white tuna in water, drained
½ cup mayonnaise
½ cup frozen whipped topping, thawed
½ cup chopped celery
¼ cup onion

1. Mix gelatins and dissolve in boiling water.
2. Add chicken noodle soup.
3. Put into 8" × 8" baking dish.
4. Chill, but do not set.
5. Mix together tuna, mayonnaise, topping, celery, and onion.
6. Add to gelatin mixture. Refrigerate until set.

Serves 6 to 9

Spinach Salad

Summertime is a good time to fix gelatin salads. Try this refreshing recipe sometime.

6 ounces lemon gelatin

2 cups boiling water

1 cup cold water

3 tablespoons vinegar

3 tablespoons mayonnaise

½ teaspoon salt

Dash pepper

2 cups cottage cheese

1 16-ounce package frozen spinach, thawed and drained well

1 cup chopped celery

4 tablespoons minced onion

1 cup frozen whipped topping, thawed

1. Dissolve gelatin in boiling water.
2. When dissolved, add cold water.
3. Chill for 20 minutes.
4. Add vinegar, mayonnaise, salt, and pepper to gelatin and beat with electric mixer until blended.
5. Add cottage cheese and beat until fluffy.
6. Add spinach, celery, and onion.
7. Fold in whipped topping.
8. Pour into 9" × 13" dish.
9. Refrigerate for 3 to 4 hours.

 Serves 12 to 15

Linda's Potato and Green Bean Salad

This recipe is from my dear friend Linda, whom I have known for over forty years. How did we get that old? She lives in Virginia, but we still keep in touch, and she sent this summer salad recipe for me to share with you in my book.

1 pound Yukon Gold or red potatoes, peeled and cut into ¾" cubes

2 cups fresh green beans, ends trimmed

¼ cup olive oil

2 tablespoons whole-grain Dijon mustard or other grainy mustard

2 tablespoons cider vinegar

2 tablespoons chopped fresh chives

2 tablespoons crumbled gorgonzola cheese

1. Cook potatoes in a large pot of boiling water for about 5 minutes.
2. Add the beans, cook until tender, and drain.
3. In a small bowl, whisk together olive oil, mustard, and vinegar.
4. Pour over beans and potatoes.
5. Chill.
6. Just before serving, add the chives and crumbled gorgonzola.
7. Gently toss.

Serves 6 to 8

Applesauce Salad

This is one of my sister-in-law Gayle's favorite gelatin recipes. If you like Red Hots, you'll love the flavor of this applesauce salad. She always made it for our children when they went to visit during the summer. They're fortunate to have such a terrific aunt.

1 3-ounce package cherry gelatin
1 cup boiling hot water
¼ cup Red Hots
1 16-ounce jar applesauce

1. Dissolve gelatin in hot water.
2. Add Red Hots and dissolve.
3. Add applesauce and stir well. Put in 8" × 8" square dish.
4. Refrigerate until set.

Serves 6 to 9

And all they of the land came to a wood;
and there was honey upon the ground.

—1 Samuel 14:25 A

7-Up Salad

Whoever thought gelatin with 7-Up would taste so good? The marshmallows and whipped topping give this a dessert-type feel, but it can be used as an accompaniment to dinner as well.

2 3-ounce packages lemon gelatin
2 cups boiling water
2 cups 7-Up
1 16-ounce package mini marshmallows
1 20-ounce can crushed pineapple, drained
1 cup pineapple juice
2 tablespoons butter
2 tablespoons flour
1 egg
1 cup sugar
1 8-ounce container frozen whipped topping, thawed
1 cup shredded Cheddar cheese

1. Dissolve gelatin in boiling water. Add 7-Up, marshmallows, and pineapple.
2. Pour into 9" × 13" dish and refrigerate until set.
3. In small saucepan, combine juice, butter, flour, egg, and sugar. Blend with wire whisk and cook until thickened like a pudding.
4. Remove from heat, fold whipped topping into pudding mixture, and spread over gelatin. Refrigerate for 4 hours.
5. When time to serve, top with Cheddar cheese.

Serves 12 to 15

Crunchy Chinese Chicken Salad

I received this recipe from one of my former teachers, Sister Valerie, about twenty years ago. She died just recently, but whenever I make this recipe, I think of her fondly. I try to keep in touch with a few of my childhood teachers—they really appreciate it. Try to contact one of your previous teachers—they'll be thrilled to hear from you!

4 cups cooked chicken, shredded

1 head iceberg lettuce, shredded

2 tablespoons toasted sesame seeds

Dash pepper

¼ cup sunflower oil

¼ cup sesame seed oil

6 tablespoons rice vinegar

2 tablespoons sugar

1 3-ounce package ramen noodles, crushed

½ cup roasted and salted cashew pieces

1. In large bowl, combine chicken, lettuce, and sesame seeds.
2. In bowl, mix together dressing of pepper, oils, vinegar, and sugar.
3. Toss chicken salad with dressing, adding ramen noodles and nuts at last minute.

Serves 6 to 8

French Beef Salad

Grandma and Aunt Ceil used to make this recipe when I walked from school to stop to eat at Grandma's house. This was one of my favorites, although she didn't fix it too often. You can also make it with leftover roast beef.

Vegetable cooking spray

1 pound mushrooms, sliced

2 tablespoons lemon juice

Salt and pepper to taste

8 tablespoons olive oil

8 teaspoons red-wine vinegar

1 teaspoon minced jarred garlic

¼ teaspoon dry mustard

¼ teaspoon thyme

⅛ teaspoon basil

1 head romaine lettuce, torn into pieces

1 pound deli roast beef, chipped

8 ounces shredded Swiss cheese

1. Spray skillet with vegetable cooking spray and sauté mushrooms until tender.
2. Remove from heat and toss with lemon juice, salt, and pepper.
3. Set aside and cool.

continued

Spinach Salad with Mushroom Dressing

4. In small bowl, combine olive oil, vinegar, garlic, mustard, thyme, and basil.
5. Put lettuce in large bowl. Add mushrooms, beef, and cheese.
6. Pour dressing over salad and toss well.

Serves 6 to 8

> *He that hath a bountiful eye shall be blessed; for he giveth of his bread to the poor.*
>
> *—Proverbs 22:9*

The mushroom dressing makes this spinach salad an outstanding one. It takes just a few minutes to fix and is good all year round. My good friend West is so good at creating new dishes and he shared this salad with me.

1 pound sliced fresh mushrooms

1½ teaspoons poppy seeds

¾ cup white or red vinegar

1½ cups oil

¾ cup sugar

1½ tablespoons chopped green onion

1½ teaspoons salt

¾ teaspoon dry mustard

1 pound bacon

1 5-ounce package spinach

1 head lettuce

2 8-ounce packages shredded Swiss cheese

1. In small bowl, combine first eight ingredients to make dressing.
2. Refrigerate dressing until ready to serve.
3. Fry bacon in skillet until crisp. Drain on paper towels to remove grease.
4. Combine spinach, lettuce, cheese, and bacon in large bowl. Toss with dressing.

Serves 6 to 8

Cole Slaw

This is a one-bowl dish that provides you with a crunchy sweet-sour taste. It's sure to become a regular on your summer menu. It's such a quick recipe to use and serves so many that you can have it for those times when you have little or no notice.

2 16-ounce packages of cole slaw
1 cup chopped onion
1 cup and 2 tablespoons sugar
1 teaspoon dry mustard
1 teaspoon celery seed
1 teaspoon salt
1 cup vinegar
¾ cup vegetable oil

1. In large bowl, put cole slaw and onions.
2. Sprinkle 1 cup sugar over cabbage and onion and toss.
3. Combine 2 tablespoons sugar, mustard, celery seed, salt, vinegar, and oil and heat to boiling.
4. Pour over cabbage mixture and refrigerate overnight.
5. Stir before serving.

Serves 16

Lois's Yummy Salad

Lois used to make this salad on every holiday occasion when we got together. I haven't had it for years, but seeing this recipe once again reminds me of the good times we shared and are still sharing. I am blessed with three fantastic sisters—Anita, Lois, and Marilyn. We're always calling each other for recipes—some new ones and old ones we can't seem to find.

1 3-ounce box lime gelatin
1 3-ounce box lemon gelatin
2 cups boiling water
1½ cups cold water
¾ cup chopped pecans
1 20-ounce can crushed pineapple, drained
1 3-ounce package cream cheese, softened
4 ounces frozen whipped topping, thawed
1½ cups pineapple juice
1 cup sugar
3 tablespoons flour
1 tablespoon lemon juice
3 eggs, beaten well

1. Dissolve gelatins in boiling water. Add cold water.
2. Add pecans and crushed pineapple. Put in 9" × 13" dish. Refrigerate until set.

continued

(Lois's Yummy Salad—continued)

3. Beat together cream cheese and whipped topping. Spread on set gelatin. Refrigerate for 20 minutes.
4. Combine pineapple juice, sugar, flour, lemon juice, and eggs and cook until thickened.
5. Put on top of cream cheese mixture when cool.
6. Let set 24 hours.

❧ Serves 12 to 15

He should have fed them also with the finest of the wheat: and with honey out of the rock should I have satisfied thee.

—Psalms 81:16

Pickled Noodles

This is a funny name for such a good dish. It's basically a pasta salad and pasta is so popular these days. It's amazing how good the pasta is with the crunchy cucumbers. It's one of my favorite salads that my friend Sharon shared with me.

1 pound rigatoni

2 cups sugar

1 teaspoon pepper

2 teaspoons prepared mustard

1 tablespoon salt

2½ cups cider vinegar

1 teaspoon garlic powder

1 finely chopped onion

1 finely chopped unpeeled cucumber

1 teaspoon jarred minced garlic

1. Cook pasta according to directions on package.
2. Drain well and rinse with cold water. Drain again.
3. In saucepan, combine sugar, pepper, mustard, salt, vinegar, and garlic powder and heat until sugar dissolves.
4. Put pasta in large bowl.
5. Add onion, cucumber, and garlic to pasta.
6. Pour dressing over mixture and toss. Cover and refrigerate at least 24 hours.

❧ Serves 8 to 10

Vinegar and Oil Potato Salad

You won't have to worry about taking this salad for a picnic since it has no mayonnaise in it. It's made with a vinegar and oil dressing and will hold up during a hot summer day.

2 15-ounce cans green beans, drained
4 cups cooked potatoes, cubed
2 green onions, sliced
¼ cup oil
2 tablespoons white wine vinegar
1 teaspoon jarred minced garlic
½ cup sliced red onion
¼ cup oil
½ teaspoon oregano, or to taste
1 teaspoon salt
⅛ teaspoon pepper

1. Mix together green beans, potatoes, and onions in medium bowl.
2. Combine remaining ingredients in small bowl and pour over vegetables. Toss gently and mix well.
3. Cover and chill for a few hours.

Serves 4 to 6

Spinach-Bacon Salad

I received this recipe from another Navy wife when we first moved to Long Beach, California. It was the first time I had ever had fresh spinach in a salad, and spinach salads are some of my favorites today.

8 bacon slices
1 16-ounce package fresh spinach
3 hard cooked eggs
¾ cup French dressing

French Dressing:
3 tablespoons cider vinegar, wine vinegar, or lemon juice
9 tablespoons olive or salad oil
1 teaspoon salt
Freshly ground pepper
Dash Tabasco
6 cloves garlic, quartered

1. Two hours ahead, make dressing by combining vinegar, oil, salt, pepper, Tabasco, and garlic.
2. Fry bacon over low heat until crisp and drain on paper towel.
3. In salad bowl, tear spinach into pieces.
4. Chop eggs and crumble bacon.
5. Sprinkle both over spinach.
6. Remove garlic from French dressing, and then pour dressing over salad.
7. Toss and serve.

Serves 6

Cranberry Chicken Salad

Gayle raved so much about her good friend Sylvia's chicken salad, I just had to try it for myself. Make this to take to your next bridge party for lots of compliments. One taste and I know why she raved about it so.

1 cup mayonnaise

1 16-ounce can jellied cranberry sauce

½ teaspoon celery seed

2 cups shell macaroni, cooked and drained

1 tablespoon minced green onion

2 cups diced cooked chicken

1 cup seedless grapes, halved

½ cup cashews

1. In small bowl, mix together mayonnaise, cranberry sauce, and celery seed.
2. In medium bowl, combine macaroni, onion, chicken, grapes, and cashews.
3. Toss macaroni chicken mixture with cranberry mixture.
4. Refrigerate until time to serve.

🐦 Serves 4 to 6

Homemade Cucumber Salad

My niece Janene's mother-in-law sends this salad home with Janene when she and Ron visit her in Pennsylvania. Janene says that everything Mary makes is made with lots of love put into it. Don't forget to make a cup of love one of your special ingredients.

7 cups unpeeled cucumbers

2 medium yellow onions, sliced

1 finely diced red pepper

1 tablespoon salt

1 cup white vinegar

2 cups sugar

1 tablespoon celery seed

1. Wash cucumbers and slice very thin.
2. In large bowl, gently toss cucumber, onions, and red pepper with salt.
3. Refrigerate overnight.
4. Drain cucumber mixture and pat dry.
5. Mix vinegar, sugar, and celery seed in microwaveable dish for about 20 to 30 seconds or until sugar is completely dissolved.
6. Return to bowl and toss with dressing.

🐦 Makes 9 cups

Soups and Stews

Flying Mom

*E*ver fly with a toddler? It can be quite an experience! More than thirty years ago, my husband, Larry, our one-year-old son, Tim, and I set out on a memorable commercial airline flight from San Francisco to Indianapolis. Our son was allowed to sit on our laps during the flight, thereby saving us the cost of a third passenger fare. Thus, we took two of the three seats next to the aisle, with the third seat being occupied by an elderly woman sitting by the window.

Although caring for and entertaining a toddler can be a challenge under any circumstances, it is especially taxing some five miles high in cramped quarters. During the four-hour flight, our son slept some, squirmed some, stood up on our laps and played some, and tried to grab our co-passenger at every opportunity whenever she was within reach. Notwithstanding this tense and tiring situation, everything went fine until it was time for the passengers to be served their meals. (Remember those long-ago years when three-course meals were even part of the economy flight package?) Tim, now fully alert and not missing any opportunity, was able to upset my salad on the lap of the passenger in the window seat. Horrors!

I immediately apologized and tried to help clean up the mess, noticing that French salad dressing was now part of the passenger's dress. After it was all said and done, the lady was quite calm and exceptionally understanding. She mentioned that she was on her way to visit her children and grandchildren, and that as accidents go, this was a very minor one. She refused our offer to reimburse her for any cleaning costs and took a turn holding Tim while he bounced in her lap. In the end, a near disaster turned into a pleasant and heartwarming experience.

Chicken Tortilla Soup

My good friend and neighbor April's 12-year-old daughter, Julie, liked this soup so much when she had it at her teacher's house that she asked her for the recipe. Her teacher willingly shared it with her. You can even make it spicier with hot salsa instead of medium salsa.

1 14.5-ounce can chicken broth
2 14.5-ounce cans tomatoes with green chilies
1 16-ounce jar salsa, medium
1 10.3-ounce can Cheddar cheese soup
1 10.3-ounce can pepper jack cheese soup
1 16-ounce package Velveeta cheese, sliced
2 cups cooked chicken, shredded

1. Combine all ingredients except chicken in Crock-Pot.
2. Cook several hours.
3. Shred chicken and add to Crock-Pot. Warm for 30 minutes.

Makes 14 to 16 cups

Tortilla Chili Casserole

Give everyone's taste buds a spicy treat for a change. I like to make this using 1 pound hot sausage and 1 pound ground beef instead of the 2 pounds ground beef. I adapted this from one of my niece Pam's recipes.

2 pounds lean ground beef
1 14.5-ounce can Chili beans
1 11-ounce bag corn chips or tortilla chips
1 pint sour cream
½ head lettuce, shredded or thinly sliced
¾ pound shredded Mexican cheese
3 cups chopped tomatoes
1 bunch small green onions
1 4.5-ounce can sliced black olives

1. Brown ground beef in skillet.
2. Drain if necessary.
3. Add canned chili mix and heat until bubbling.
4. Reduce heat, keep warm, and allow to simmer gently a few minutes.
5. In greased 9" × 13" dish, place layer of corn chips topped with chili.
6. Spread with sour cream. Add lettuce, shredded cheese, tomatoes, green onions, and black olives. Serve immediately.

Serves 8 to 10

Butternut Soup

You can make this with fresh squash, and I have done so for many years. But ever since I found the squash already prepared, in the freezer section at my grocery store, I use that. And it tastes just as good.

1 tablespoon olive oil
3 10-ounce packages frozen squash, thawed
1 medium onion, chopped
1 teaspoon jarred minced garlic
½ teaspoon ground allspice
2 14.5-ounce cans chicken broth
½ cup sour cream
Saltine crackers

1. Heat oil in large saucepan on medium heat.
2. Add squash, onion, and garlic; cook for 5 minutes, stirring occasionally.
3. Add allspice; cook, stirring, for 1 minute.
4. Add chicken broth and bring to boil.
5. Cover and reduce heat to low.
6. Add sour cream.
7. Simmer 15 minutes.
8. Serve with crackers.

Serves 8

Chicken, Cheese, and Broccoli Soup

My southern cooking friend, Ellen, sent me this recipe. I tried it using just boneless chicken breasts and I liked it because it was a little easier.

One fryer, 1½ to 2 pounds
Water to cover the chicken
1 cup chopped green peppers
1 cup chopped red peppers
½ cup chopped onion
½ cup chopped carrots
Salt and pepper
1 bay leaf
½ pound egg noodles
1 16-ounce package frozen broccoli, thawed
1 quart milk
½ to 1 quart chicken broth
1 pound Velveeta cheese, cubed

1. In a big pot, cover chicken with water; add all the vegetables except the broccoli along with the salt, pepper, and bay leaf.
2. Bring to a boil, then simmer about 40 to 50 minutes, until meat falls off the bones.
3. When chicken is done, lift it out to cool, deskin, cut into bite-size pieces, and debone.

continued

(Chicken, Cheese, and Broccoli Soup—continued)

4. While chicken is cooling, add enough water so you have about 8 cups of water and return to a boil.
5. Add the noodles; boil for 2 minutes, then add the broccoli.
6. Cook for 10 to 15 minutes
7. Add the milk and Velveeta cheese and warm until cheese melts.
8. Adjust seasonings. Add the chicken.
9. Bring back to serving temperature.

Makes 12 cups

Then he said unto him,
Come home with me, and eat bread.

—1 Kings 13:15

Mystery Stew

I have always enjoyed my sister Anita's home cooking. She's a superb cook and for as many years as I can remember, she has always had big family dinners on Sunday. You'll enjoy this stew of hers, I'm sure, although it's a mystery to me why she named it mystery stew.

2 pounds ground turkey
2 cups diced celery
1 cup chopped onion
4 cups tomato juice
1 1.25-ounce package chili seasoning mix
2 16-ounce cans French-cut green beans
1 14.5-ounce can diced carrots, drained
1 10-ounce package frozen corn, thawed

1. Brown celery and onion with the ground turkey.
2. Drain and add turkey mixture to tomato juice in large pan.
3. Add seasoning mix and enough water to make slightly soupy.
4. Bring to a boil and simmer about 15 minutes.
5. Add green beans, carrots, and corn.
6. Simmer for 15 minutes more.

Makes 6 to 8 cups

Cheddar Chowder

My children used to love "cheese soup," as they call it, and this was one of their favorites. This soup is one of the few ways I can get one of my daughters to eat vegetables, so I double the carrots and the celery given in this recipe.

2 cups boiling water
2 cups chopped potatoes
½ cup chopped carrots
½ cup chopped celery
¼ cup chopped onion
1 cup ham, cut into cubes
¼ cup margarine
2 cups milk
¼ cup flour
2 cups shredded Cheddar cheese

1. In large pan, combine water, vegetables, and ham.
2. Cover and simmer 10 to 20 minutes or until vegetables are tender.
3. In saucepan, melt margarine and add flour; stir until bubbly.
4. Gradually add milk with wire whisk and stir until thickened.
5. Add cheese and stir until melted.
6. Pour into vegetable and ham mixture.
7. Heat for 10 minutes.

Makes 6 to 8 cups

I am the living bread which came down from heaven: if any man eat of this bread, he shall live for ever: and the bread that I will give is my flesh, which I will give for the life of the world.

—John 6:51

Cincinnati Chili in a Dish

Here in Ohio, everyone knows about Cincinnati's famous chili. There are a couple of restaurants that offer it on their hot dogs and spaghetti, with your choice of onion, beans, and cheese, any combination you want. Thanks, Annis, for this casserole that is close to the original Cincinnati chili.

1 pound ground beef

1 chopped onion

1 16-ounce can tomatoes

1 16-ounce can kidney beans

1 teaspoon garlic powder

1 or 2 dashes pepper

1½ teaspoons ground cloves

¼ teaspoon salt

Few drops of Tabasco sauce

1 teaspoon cinnamon

8 ounces cooked angel hair pasta, drained

2 cups shredded Cheddar cheese

1 cup chopped onions

1. Brown beef with onions. Drain well.
2. Put in large pan and add remaining ingredients except for last three; simmer for 45 to 60 minutes.
3. Stir chili frequently.
4. Adjust seasoning to taste.
5. Place pasta in greased 9" × 13" baking dish. Top with chili. Sprinkle cheese on top of chili and add onions on top of cheese.
6. Cover with foil and keep warm in 250° oven until served.

Serves 6 to 8

And when the dew fell upon the camp in the night, the manna fell upon it.

—Numbers 11:9

Potato Soup au Gratin

You can spice up this soup even more by substituting a 16-ounce jar of hot salsa in place of the tomato and green chilies. I use this recipe "as is"—it's just hot enough for my family.

1 4.9-ounce package Betty Crocker au gratin potatoes

1 10-ounce package frozen corn, thawed

1 14.5-ounce can diced tomatoes with green chilies, undrained

1½ cups water

1 stick margarine

2 cups milk

2 cups cubed processed American cheese

1. In a saucepan, combine the package of au gratin potatoes and sauce mix with corn, tomatoes, green chilies, water, and margarine.
2. Mix well.
3. Bring to a boil.
4. Reduce heat; cover and simmer for 15 to 18 minutes or until potatoes are tender.
5. Add milk and cheese.
6. Cook and stir until cheese melts. Serve with tortilla chips.

Makes 8 to 10 cups

Creamy Corn Chowder

I love to make this soup with red peppers, as they seem to taste sweeter when they simmer in this "soup pot." This is even more American than apple pie.

1 cup chopped onions

½ cup chopped red bell pepper

½ teaspoon of minced jarred garlic

1 tablespoon butter or margarine

2 medium peeled and cut potatoes, cut into ½" cubes

2 14.5-ounce cans chicken broth

1 15-ounce can cream-style corn

¼ teaspoon pepper

½ cup half-and-half

1 tablespoon chopped parsley

1. Combine onion, bell pepper, garlic, and butter in skillet and cook until tender.
2. Add potatoes, chicken broth, corn, and pepper to mixture.
3. Cook, stirring occasionally, on medium heat for 30 to 40 minutes or until potatoes are tender.
4. Stir in half-and-half until heated through.
5. Sprinkle with parsley and serve.

Serves 6 to 8

Tortilla Chili

I don't add the tortilla chips when I take this to a carry-in. Instead, I crush some tortilla chips and take them in a bowl along with bowls of Cheddar cheese and sour cream. Then everyone can put in their own chips, cheese, and sour cream if they wish. Works out well.

2 pounds of boneless, skinless chicken breast, cut into bite-size pieces
2 1.25-ounce packages chili seasoning mix
2 14.5-ounce cans diced tomatoes
1 15-ounce can pinto beans, juice and all
2 15.25-ounce cans Mexican-style corn, drained
2 cups water
2 cups broken tortilla chips

1. Heat a lightly oiled large skillet over medium high heat.
2. Add chicken. Cook and stir for about 5 minutes, until lightly browned.
3. Stir in remaining ingredients except tortilla chips and bring to a boil.
4. Reduce heat to low.
5. Cover and simmer for 15 minutes, stirring occasionally. Mix in tortilla chips.
6. Serve with shredded Cheddar cheese and sour cream, if desired.

Serves 10

Veggie Chili with Beef

This is a really fast chili you can have ready to go in less than an hour. I double or triple the recipe when I take it for a crowd.

1 28-ounce can tomato sauce
1 pound ground beef, browned and drained
1 15-ounce can mixed vegetables, with liquid
1 16-ounce can kidney beans, drained and rinsed
1 14.5-ounce can diced whole tomatoes
2 teaspoons chili powder
Shredded Cheddar cheese
¾ cup diced green onions
Corn chips

1. In 3-quart saucepan, combine all ingredients except Cheddar cheese, onions, and corn chips.
2. Bring to a boil. Reduce heat, cover, and simmer for 20 to 30 minutes, stirring occasionally.
3. Serve hot with shredded cheese, diced green onions, and corn chips as toppers.

Serves 8

Sweet Chili

If you like your barbecue sauce on the sweet side, you may like this sweet yet spicy chili. I'm a fan of sweet barbecue sauce, and I really like the taste of this chili.

1 pound ground beef
1 tablespoon chili powder
1 teaspoon ketchup
1 16-ounce can kidney beans
1 16-ounce can chili beans
½ cup brown sugar
1 6-ounce can tomato paste
1 10.75-ounce can tomato soup

1. Brown hamburger with a pinch of chili powder and ketchup.
2. Mix all ingredients in Crock-Pot and let simmer for a minimum of 2 hours.

Serves 6 to 8

Pepper's Tomato Soup

Nothing says comfort food like this classic tomato soup that Pepper has shared with me. Be sure to make grilled cheese sandwiches using thickly sliced bread to serve with this delicious soup.

1 quart milk
1 28-ounce can diced tomatoes
Dash salt
½ teaspoon baking soda
2 tablespoons butter

1. Heat milk to scalding in medium saucepan.
2. Add tomatoes, dash salt, and baking soda and stir until smooth.
3. Stir in butter.

Serves 6

Chicken Dumpling Soup

This palate-pleasing soup brings back wonderful memories of supper around the table. Dad and Mom eager to hear of our day's happenings and each of the four of us wanting to speak all at the same time. Just the smell of this soup brings those memories back as though it were happening right now. I'm sure you must have certain nostalgic recipes of yours. Great feeling, isn't it!

8 cups chicken broth
2 16-ounce bags frozen stew vegetables
½ teaspoon onion powder
½ teaspoon garlic powder
2 beaten eggs
2 cups flour
¼ teaspoon salt
3 5-ounce cans chicken breast

1. Heat chicken broth large pot until it comes to a boil.
2. Add frozen vegetables and seasonings.
3. Simmer for ten minutes.
4. Put flour in medium bowl.
5. Dip fork into flour and add eggs to flour. Mix eggs and flour together until the mixture forms little dumplings.
6. Add chicken to soup, bringing soup back to boiling.
7. Take tiny spoonfuls of dumplings and add to boiling broth. Boil soup for three minutes.
8. Turn heat down and simmer for five more minutes.

Makes 12 cups

And the manna ceased on the morrow after they had eaten of the old corn of the land; neither had the children of Israel manna any more; but they did eat of the fruit of the land of Canaan that year.

—Joshua 5:12

Curried Chicken Soup

My sister Lois dearly loves a soup at a little restaurant in a small town in Indiana. I've tried to make it after tasting some she brought me. This is not quite the same, but we both like it—and it is low in calories as well!

1 tablespoon butter or margarine
½ cup finely chopped onion
½ cup finely chopped carrots
½ cup finely chopped celery
¼ cup flour
5 cups chicken broth
1 cup unsweetened applesauce
2 teaspoons sugar substitute
1 teaspoon curry powder
1 10-ounce can cooked chicken breast, drained

1. Melt butter in skillet and sauté onions, carrots, and celery until tender over medium heat.
2. Blend in flour and cook until bubbly.
3. Transfer veggie mixture to Dutch oven and add broth; bring to a boil, lower heat, and cook for 30 minutes.
4. Add remaining ingredients.
5. Cook over low heat for an additional 10 minutes.

Makes 6 cups

Mom's Mashed Potato Soup

I had to make this recipe since I wanted to include it for you. You know how it is with some recipes—you just throw a little bit of this in, add some of that, etc., but you never can tell others the exact proportions. This soup thickens as it simmers, so you may want to add some more milk.

2½ pounds potatoes
¼ pound carrots
1½ sticks celery
1 whole onion, peeled
¾ stick margarine
3¼ cups milk

1. Peel and dice potatoes. Place in 5-quart pan and cover with water.
2. Add carrots, celery, and onion.
3. Cook over medium heat until potatoes are tender.
4. Drain potatoes and remove carrots, celery, and onion.
5. Put potatoes back into pan and mash by hand.
6. Add ¼ stick margarine and ¼ cup of milk and beat with electric mixer.
7. After making mashed potatoes, gradually add 3 cups milk and ½ stick of margarine to potatoes.
8. Serve warm with butter. Soup will thicken as it sets, so when reheating, add milk as needed.

Makes 9 cups

Sweet Things

Hot Coffee

*W*ay back in my high school days, my girlfriend Patsy's parents owned a catering business. They were doing a big sit-down dinner and needed some extra help serving. They asked me and some other friends if we would be willing to help. It sounded like fun, so we were given some instructions on serving etiquette and off we went.

Everything seemed to go well until dessert time. As I was pouring coffee for one gentleman, making sure to pour on the correct side as I had just learned to do, a couple of drops of coffee splashed on his hand. He became very angry. I apologized profusely and asked him if he was burned. Fortunately, he wasn't, as the coffee was not that hot. I then decided to make sure I still had enough coffee in the coffeepot to continue serving. As I stood behind him, instead of opening the lid to see, I shook the coffee pot to see how full it was. I guess I must have done it vigorously because some coffee came out and splashed the back of his suit. Well, young and foolish as I was, I quickly looked to see if anyone had noticed, especially him. Since he seemed to be completely unaware of it, I quickly retreated to the kitchen, keeping my mouth shut and deciding to let him find out on his own. I stayed in the kitchen and didn't come out until all the guests had left. Needless to say, I never served coffee again.

Unbelievably Good Candy

All of us were surprised at how easy and scrumptious this recipe was when we tried it for the first time. We ate it so quickly that we had to make another batch the next day to share with other family and friends. Thanks, Anita.

1 sleeve saltine crackers, approximately 40

2 sticks margarine

1 cup sugar

6 ounces Reese's peanut butter cups, chopped

6 ounces chocolate chips

1. Line cookie sheet with foil.
2. Place saltines end to end and fill in any spaces with pieces of saltines.
3. Melt margarine and add sugar in medium saucepan.
4. Boil for 3 minutes.
5. Pour over crackers.
6. Bake at 400° for 7 minutes.
7. Mix together chocolate chips and peanut butter cups.
8. Remove from oven and spread chocolate chips and peanut butter cups over crackers.
9. Chill for 30 minutes and break into pieces.

Makes 40 pieces

Aunt Susan's Brown Candy

This is one of Lois's favorite candy recipes. She and I made it together a couple of years ago. She's right when she recommends that two people work together on this, as the iron skillet gets pretty heavy with the candy in it.

6 cups sugar

2 cups whole milk

½ teaspoon baking soda

¼ pound butter or margarine

1 teaspoon vanilla

2 16-ounce packages pecans

1. Pour 2 cups sugar into heavy iron skillet and place over low heat.
2. Begin stirring with wooden spoon and keep sugar moving so it won't scorch.
3. It will take about ½ hour to melt sugar, and it will be the color of light brown sugar syrup.
4. In the meantime, pour 4 cups sugar together with milk into heavy kettle and set on low heat to cook slowly, bringing it to a boil.
5. As soon as sugar is melted, begin pouring it into kettle of boiling milk, keeping it on low heat, stirring constantly.
6. Continue cooking and stirring until a bit of the mixture forms a firm ball (244° to 248°) when dropped in cold water.
7. Remove from heat and add soda, stirring vigorously as it foams.

continued

Fluffer Nutter Candy

8. As soon as soda is mixed in, add butter.
9. Let cool for 20 minutes and add vanilla, and begin beating with wooden spoon until thick and heavy. It should have a dull appearance instead of glossy sheen.
10. Add pecan pieces.
11. Pour into greased dish and cut into squares when cooled.

Makes 5 pounds

And he took butter, and milk, and the calf which he had dressed, and set it before them; and he stood by them under the tree, and they did eat.

—Genesis 18:8

Remember making fluffer nutter sandwiches with peanut butter? This recipe reminds me of the marshmallow–peanut butter sandwiches I used to make for the kids when they were little. It's easy to make, and it won't last long once the kids get a taste of it.

2 6-ounce packages semisweet chocolate pieces
1 cup crunchy peanut butter
4 cups miniature marshmallows

1. Melt chocolate with peanut butter in saucepan over low heat; stir until smooth.
2. Fold in marshmallows.
3. Pour into greased 9" square dish.
4. Chill until firm.
5. Cut into squares.

Makes 20 pieces

Ohio Buckeyes

Buckeyes are a very popular candy here in Ohio, the Buckeye State. The peanut butter and chocolate are a winning combination. You can use crunchy peanut butter in place of the creamy peanut butter for a little crunch.

2 16-ounce jars peanut butter
1 pound margarine, softened
3 pounds powdered sugar
24 ounces chocolate chips
1 square of paraffin

1. Mix peanut butter, margarine, and powdered sugar and form into balls and refrigerate overnight.
2. Melt chocolate chips and cake of paraffin in bowl in microwave for 1 minute. Remove, stir, and repeat until completely melted.
3. Using a toothpick, dip peanut butter balls in chocolate, leaving a circle uncovered on top.
4. Place on waxed paper and store in airtight container when chocolate is completely dry.

Makes 200

No-Cook Mint Patties

If your sweet tooth is getting the better of you, you can make these patties and enjoy them in just a few hours. You don't have to have a special occasion to make them—make them just because. Thanks, Lois.

1/3 cup light corn syrup
1/4 cup butter, softened
1 teaspoon mint flavoring
1/2 teaspoon salt
1 16-ounce box powdered sugar
Red and green food coloring

1. Blend corn syrup, butter, mint flavoring, and salt.
2. Add sugar and mix with spoon and hands until smooth.
3. Divide into thirds.
4. Knead 1 drop green food coloring into first third. Knead 1 drop red food coloring into second third.
5. Leave remaining third white.
6. Shape into small balls.
7. Flatten with fork on waxed paper lined baking sheets.
8. Let dry several hours.
9. Store in an airtight container.

Makes 72

Bonbons

I was looking through my recipes and couldn't find the bonbon recipe that my sister Marilyn and I used to make frequently. I called her, and luckily she still had it. It had been so long since she'd made them that she'd forgotten about them. *You* won't forget about these once you try them.

1 14-ounce can sweetened condensed milk

2 16-ounce packages powdered sugar

1 stick margarine or butter, softened

1 cup fine coconut flakes

2 cups finely chopped pecans

2 16-ounce packages chocolate chips

2 tablespoons butter

1. Mix all ingredients except chocolate chips and 2 tablespoons butter together and roll into 1" balls.
2. Set on wax paper. Chill for 1 hour.
3. Melt chocolate chips and butter in small bowl in microwave for 1 minute. Remove and stir. Microwave for 30 seconds more and stir again.
4. Repeat at 30 second intervals until chocolate is melted. Be careful not to burn chocolate.
5. Put toothpick into ball and dip in chocolate and place on wax paper to set.
6. Store in airtight container when chocolate is completely dry.

꼬 Makes 125 1" balls

Peanut Butter Pinwheels

My friend Georgia used to make a peanut butter divinity pinwheel that was out of this world. I helped her a time or two, but it was a lot of work to make the divinity. When I tried this easy recipe for divinity that is almost as good as Georgia's, I had to run some samples over to her to taste. We were both thrilled that Annis gave me this recipe.

1 16-ounce can vanilla ready-to-serve frosting

1 pound powdered sugar

½ cup to 1 cup peanut butter

1. Put frosting in large bowl and combine with powdered sugar.
2. Knead powdered sugar into frosting until it is stiff. Divide mixture into 4 balls.
3. Roll out ball mixture on wax paper sprinkled with powdered sugar. Roll into 9" × 8" rectangle.
4. Spread thin layer of peanut butter over frosting mixture.
5. Roll up like jelly roll.
6. Wrap in wax paper and chill. Repeat for remaining rolls.
7. Slice and put in airtight container with wax paper between layers.

꼬 Makes 48

White Chocolate Party Mix

This is one of my favorite treats to make during the Christmas season. I like to give them as gifts to teachers, friends, and neighbors for the holidays. A couple of my friends found it so addictive that they were making it every other day. Be careful—you'll love it too.

2 cups Wheat Chex

2 cups Rice Chex

2 cups Corn Chex

2 cups Cheerios

2 cups pretzel sticks, broken into pieces

4 cups roasted and salted peanuts

1 16-ounce package mini M&Ms, optional

2 pounds white chocolate or 3 12-ounce packages of white chocolate chips

1. In a large bowl, combine the cereals, pretzels, and nuts.
2. In microwave-safe bowl, heat white chocolate for 2 minutes on medium setting. Remove and stir if necessary and put back in microwave for 30 seconds.
3. Remove and stir until smooth.
4. Pour over cereal mixture. Mix until coated.
5. Spread waxed paper on table top or baking sheet and spread mixture onto waxed paper.
6. When it is cool and has hardened, break apart and store in airtight container.

❧ Makes 4 quarts

Hot Fudge Pudding Cake

This moist and chocolaty cake has a decadent taste. Be sure to take along a container of whipped topping to serve with this rich cake.

1 cup flour

¾ cup sugar

2 tablespoons cocoa

2 teaspoons baking powder

¼ teaspoon salt

½ cup milk

2 tablespoons vegetable oil

1 teaspoon vanilla

1 cup chopped nuts

1 cup packed brown sugar

¼ cup cocoa

1¼ cups hot water

1. Heat oven to 350°.
2. Mix flour, sugar, 2 tablespoons cocoa, baking powder, and salt in ungreased 9" × 9" baking dish.
3. Mix in milk, oil, and vanilla with fork until smooth.
4. Stir in nuts and spread in dish.
5. Mix together brown sugar and cocoa. Sprinkle over cake mixture.
6. Pour hot water over batter.
7. Bake 40 minutes.
8. Let stand 15 minutes.

❧ Serves 9

Zucchini Cake

Summer brings an abundance of zucchini if you have a lot of friends who grow it in their gardens. This is a somewhat healthy way to satisfy your sweet tooth and get your daily quota of veggies. Share one with those who share their garden veggies with you.

1½ cups oil

4 tablespoons hot water

2 cups sugar

1½ cups grated zucchini

2½ cups flour

3 teaspoons baking powder

1 teaspoon salt

1 teaspoon vanilla

1 teaspoon cinnamon

½ teaspoon nutmeg

4 eggs, separated

Confectioners' sugar

1. Mix together all ingredients except egg whites and confectioner's sugar in a large bowl. Beat for 2 minutes.
2. Beat egg whites until stiff and fold into rest of mix.
3. Pour into greased and floured bundt cake pan.
4. Bake at 350° for 45 minutes.
5. Cool and remove from pan. Sprinkle with confectioners' sugar.

🍃 Serves 14 to 16

Bev's Oatmeal Chocolate Chip Cake

My sister-in-law Gayle told me to include this cake as it is one of her favorites. I want to keep in her good graces, so here it is. Her friend Bev gave it to her.

1¾ cups boiling water

1 cup uncooked oatmeal

1 cup lightly packed brown sugar

1 cup granulated sugar

½ cup margarine

2 large eggs

1¾ cups flour

1 teaspoon baking soda

½ teaspoon salt

1 tablespoon cocoa

1 24-ounce package chocolate chips

¾ cup chopped walnuts

1. Pour boiling water over oatmeal.
2. Let stand at room temperature for 10 minutes.
3. Add both sugars and margarine.
4. Add eggs and beat.
5. Add flour, soda, salt, and cocoa and mix well.
6. Add half the chocolate chips and blend in.
7. Pour batter into greased 9" × 13" baking dish.
8. Sprinkle remaining chocolate chips and walnuts over top.
9. Bake 35 to 40 minutes in 350° oven.

🍃 Serves 24

Strawberry Cake

This used to be one of my sister Lois's favorite cakes when she was in her cooking and baking days. For some years now she has gotten away from cooking. She tells me she wants a house without a kitchen!

1 18.25-ounce box white cake mix
1 3-ounce box strawberry gelatin
½ cup water
½ cup frozen strawberries, thawed and drained
½ cup salad oil
4 egg whites

Icing:
1 stick of butter or margarine, softened
1 16-ounce box powdered sugar
½ cup frozen strawberries, thawed and drained

1. Combine cake mix, gelatin, water, strawberries, oil, and egg whites in a bowl and beat with electric mixer for 3 minutes.
2. Bake at 350° for 35 minutes in 9" × 13" greased and floured baking dish.
3. Beat icing ingredients together well. If necessary, add some strawberry juices.
4. Frost when cake is cool.

✻ Serves 24

Cherry Chocolate Cake

I can't remember the first time Gayle made this cake and brought it for our Christmas dinner. Since then, it's been a favorite. It takes just ten minutes to make cake and icing.

1 30-ounce can cherry pie filling
1 teaspoon almond extract
2 beaten eggs
1 18.25-ounce box devil's food cake mix

Icing:
1 cup powdered sugar
5 teaspoons margarine
⅓ cup milk
1 cup chocolate chips

1. With electric beater, beat together cherry filling, almond extract, eggs, and devil's food cake mix for 2 to 3 minutes.
2. Put in greased and floured 9" × 13" baking dish.
3. Bake at 350° for 20 to 30 minutes.
4. In medium saucepan, boil sugar, margarine, and milk for 1 minute.
5. Remove from heat and add chocolate chips.
6. Pour over warm cake.

✻ Serves 15 to 18

Italian Cream Cake

My sister Lois is now 77 and still meets with her former high school friends once a month for breakfast. Her longtime friend and former classmate Theresa shared this recipe with me. Theresa's brother loves this cake and she makes it for him whenever he comes to town.

½ cup Crisco

1 stick margarine

2 cups sugar

5 egg yolks

½ teaspoon salt

2 cups flour

1 cup buttermilk

1 teaspoon baking soda

1 teaspoon vanilla

1 cup coconut

1 cup pecans

5 egg whites

Icing:

1 stick butter or margarine, softened

1 8-ounce cream cheese, softened

1 16-ounce box powdered sugar

1 cup pecan pieces

1 teaspoon vanilla flavoring

1. Cream together Crisco, margarine, and sugar.
2. Add egg yolks, one at a time.
3. Mix in salt, flour, buttermilk, baking soda, and vanilla.
4. Stir in coconut and pecans.
5. Beat egg whites until stiff and fold into batter.
6. Grease and flour 3 8" cake pans.
7. Pour batter into pans and bake at 350° for 30 minutes.
8. Beat butter and cream cheese until smooth.
9. Add powdered sugar.
10. Blend well.
11. Add pecan pieces and vanilla.
12. Frost cake when cool.

Serves 12 to 16

And he dealt to every one of Israel, both man and woman, to every one a loaf of bread, and a good piece of flesh, and a flagon of wine.

—1 Chronicles 16:3

Summer Lemon Cake

Lemon lovers, like my sister Lois, who shared this recipe with me, will love this refreshing cake, especially during the hot months. It seems like anything lemon hits the spot during the summer.

1 18.25-ounce box of lemon cake mix

1 3.4-ounce box instant lemon pudding

¾ cup salad oil

¾ cup water

4 eggs, beaten

Glaze:

3 cups powdered sugar

3 tablespoons melted butter

½ cup lemon juice

1. Combine cake mix, pudding, salad oil, water, and eggs and beat with electric mixer for 4 minutes.
2. Pour into greased and floured 9" × 13" baking dish.
3. Bake at 350° for 30 to 35 minutes.
4. Combine powdered sugar, melted butter, and lemon juice and mix until smooth.
5. While cake is still hot, punch holes over top of cake with a fork.
6. Pour glaze over hot cake.
7. Refrigerate.
8. Serve cold.

Serves 12 to 15

Laura's Yummy Apple Cake

As soon as Laura shared this recipe with me, I had to make it. She had told me how moist it was and how it was just as good a few days old. She was right, and the Baking Splenda she used worked out really well.

6 cups apples

1 cup Baking Splenda

½ cup canola oil

1 cup pecan pieces

2 eggs, well beaten

2 teaspoons vanilla

2 cups flour

2 teaspoons baking soda

2 teaspoons cinnamon

¼ teaspoon salt

1. Preheat oven to 350°.
2. Peel and dice apples and toss them with Baking Splenda in large bowl.
3. Add oil, pecans, eggs, and vanilla.
4. Mix together all dry ingredients and add to apple mixture.
5. Bake in a greased 9" × 13" baking dish for 40 minutes to 1 hour.

Serves 16

Poppy Seed Cake

Pudding has so many uses; it makes this cake rich and moist. I've substituted sugar-free pudding in this recipe and you can't tell the difference. Now, if they would just sell a sugar-free cake mix.

1 18.25-ounce package yellow cake mix
1 5.1-ounce package vanilla instant pudding
4 eggs
1 cup water
½ cup oil
¼ cup poppy seeds
Powdered sugar

1. In large bowl, beat together all ingredients for 10 minutes.
2. Pour into greased and floured bundt pan.
3. Bake for 1 hour at 350°.
4. Cool and remove from pan and dust with powdered sugar.

Serves 14 to 16

Mississippi Mud Cake

I've lost touch with Shirley, who used to make all kinds of sweet confections for my candy and catering business. This is one of the cakes she used to make; its name doesn't do it justice.

2 cups sugar
⅓ cup cocoa
1½ cups margarine
4 eggs
1 teaspoon vanilla
1½ cups flour
1⅓ cups coconut
1½ cups chopped pecans
1 7-ounce jar of marshmallow crème

Icing:
1 16-ounce box confectioners' sugar
⅓ cup cocoa
½ cup margarine
½ cup evaporated milk
1 tablespoon vanilla

1. Cream together sugar, cocoa, and margarine.
2. Add eggs, vanilla, and mix.
3. Stir in flour, coconut, and pecans.
4. Bake in a greased and floured 9" × 13" baking dish at 350° for 40 minutes.

continued

(Mississippi Mud Cake—continued)

5. Microwave marshmallow crème for 10 to 20 seconds and stir. Gently spread crème on cake.
6. Cool cake.
7. Sift together sugar and cocoa.
8. Cream margarine with cocoa mixture.
9. Beat in milk and vanilla.
10. Gently spread frosting on cake.

🍬 Serves 15 to 18

One of his disciples, Andrew, Simon Peter's brother, saith unto him, There is a lad here, which hath five barley loaves, and two small fishes: but what are they among so many?

—John 6:8–9

No-Stir Cake

I think many of you have this recipe, but just in case you don't, here it is again. It is an old standby of my sister Anita, who likes it best with cream cheese frosting.

1 30-ounce can cherry pie filling

1 20-ounce can pineapple chunks, drained

1 18.25-ounce package yellow cake mix

1 cup melted butter

1 cup shredded coconut

1 cup chopped pecans

1. Spread pie filling in a greased and floured 9" × 13" baking dish.
2. Cover with pineapple, then sprinkle cake mix on top of pineapple.
3. Drizzle butter over cake mix.
4. Sprinkle with coconut and pecans.
5. Bake at 350° for 45 minutes.
6. Turn oven down to 325° for 15 or 20 minutes.
7. Frost with prepared cream cheese frosting if desired.

🍬 Serves 15 to 18

Turtle Cake

Chocolate, caramel, and pecans—can a cake get any better than this? "Life is good, eat more chocolate" is one of my mottoes. But don't overdo it, or you'll have to worry about getting rid of those extra pounds. I know all about that.

1 18.25-ounce package chocolate cake mix

½ cup evaporated milk

¾ cup melted margarine

½ cup evaporated milk.

1 12-ounce jar caramel syrup

1 cup chopped pecans

1 cup chocolate chips

Chocolate frosting (optional)

1. In medium bowl, combine cake mix, ½ cup milk, and margarine. Spread half of batter into greased 9" × 13" baking dish.
2. Bake at 350° for 6 or 7 minutes.
3. Remove from oven.
4. Combine ½ cup evaporated milk and caramel syrup. Pour over cake.
5. Sprinkle pecans and chocolate chips over caramel mixture.
6. Bake at 350° for another 10 to 15 minutes.
7. Top with chocolate frosting if desired.

🍃 Serves 12 to 15

Ann's Fresh Apple Cake

One of my new friends, Linda, who is in a health and fitness group with me, shared her friend Ann's apple cake recipe with me. She says that this has been very popular at her church events.

3 cups diced, peeled apples

1 cup oil

1 cup brown sugar

1 cup white sugar

2 eggs

1 teaspoon vanilla

2½ cups flour

1 teaspoon salt

1½ teaspoons baking soda

2 teaspoons cinnamon

1. In large bowl, stir together apples, oil, brown sugar, white sugar, eggs, and vanilla.
2. Add flour, salt, baking soda, and cinnamon.
3. Bake in greased and floured 9" × 13" baking dish at 350° for 30 to 45 minutes.

🍃 Serves 15 to 18

Pauline's Carrot Cake

About ten years ago, I met Pauline through a mutual friend. She did a beautiful job reupholstering my sofa. When I first went to her home, she invited me to have a piece of carrot cake. It was outstanding. She willingly shared this recipe with me; it is my favorite carrot cake.

2 cups flour

1 tablespoon cinnamon

2 teaspoons baking soda

2 cups sugar

1½ cups salad oil

4 eggs

2 cups grated carrots

½ cup pecan pieces

1 20-ounce can crushed pineapple

1 teaspoon vanilla

Frosting:

1 8-ounce package cream cheese, softened

1 stick butter, softened

2¼ cups powdered sugar

1 teaspoon cream or milk

1 teaspoon vanilla

1. Sift together flour, cinnamon, and baking soda.

2. In medium bowl, blend together sugar and oil and add eggs one at a time, beating well after each.
3. Add carrots, pecans, pineapple, and vanilla.
4. Add flour mixture to batter and beat for 2 minutes.
5. Bake at 300° for 40 minutes in a greased and floured 9" × 13" baking dish.
6. Blend cream cheese and butter.
7. Add powdered sugar, milk, and vanilla.
8. Spread icing over cake when barely warm.

Serves 15 to 18

But I have said unto you, Ye shall inherit their land, and I will give it unto you to possess it, a land that floweth with milk and honey: I am the LORD your God, which have separated you from other people.

—Leviticus 20:24

Pumpkin Pound Cake with Pecan Sauce

The sauce is a perfect addition to this cake. I put it in a container and serve it when I serve the cake. Add whipped topping for a special treat.

1½ cups butter or margarine, softened

2¾ cups sugar

6 eggs

1 teaspoon vanilla extract

3 cups flour

¾ teaspoon cinnamon

½ teaspoon baking powder

½ teaspoon salt

½ teaspoon ground ginger

¼ teaspoon ground cloves

1 cup canned pumpkin

Pecan Sauce:

1 cup packed brown sugar

½ cup whipping cream

¼ cup corn syrup

2 tablespoons butter or margarine

½ cup chopped pecans

½ teaspoon vanilla extract

1. In mixing bowl, cream together butter and sugar.
2. Add eggs, one at a time, beating well after each addition.
3. Stir in vanilla.
4. Combine flour, cinnamon, baking powder, salt, ginger, and cloves. Add to creamed mixture alternately with pumpkin, beating until combined.
5. Pour into 2 greased and floured 9" × 5" × 3" loaf pans.
6. Bake at 350° for 65 to 70 minutes or until toothpick inserted near center comes out clean.
7. Cool for 10 minutes before removing from pans to wire racks to cool completely.
8. For sauce, combine brown sugar, cream, corn syrup, and butter in saucepan.
9. Bring to boil over medium heat, stirring constantly.
10. Reduce heat. Cook and stir 5 minutes longer.
11. Remove from heat. Stir in pecans and vanilla.
12. Serve warm over cake.

Serves 16

Marie's Delicious Oatmeal Cake

My friend Marie used to have her own bakery and made everything she sold. This oatmeal cake was a big seller and I was very pleased when she gave me the recipe for it.

1 cup quick cooking oatmeal

1⅓ cups boiling water

½ cup melted butter

1 cup brown sugar

1 cup white sugar

2 eggs, beaten

1½ cups flour

1 teaspoon baking soda

1 teaspoon cinnamon

1 teaspoon salt

Topping:

6 tablespoons melted butter

½ cup brown sugar

½ cup coconut

½ cup pecans

¼ cup half-and-half

½ teaspoon vanilla

1. In medium bowl, pour boiling water over oatmeal.
2. Stir and let cool.
3. Cream together butter and sugars.
4. Add eggs.
5. With electric mixer, beat creamed mixture until fluffy.
6. Sift together flour, baking soda, cinnamon, and salt and add alternately with the oatmeal to the creamed mixture until well blended.
7. Pour into greased and floured 9" × 13" baking dish.
8. Bake at 350° for 35 minutes.
9. In medium bowl, combine all ingredients for topping.
10. While cake is hot, spread topping on cake and broil 4" from broiler until mixture is bubbly. It does not take long. Keep a watchful eye on it.

Serves 15 to 18

And there came a man from Baalshalisha, and brought the man of God bread of the firstfruits, twenty loaves of barley, and full ears of corn in the husk thereof. And he said, Give unto the people, that they may eat.

—2 Kings 4:42

Grandma's Chocolate Cake

This cake that Kathi's Grandma used to make brings back wonderful memories of the days when she used to go to Grandma and Grandpa's farm for a visit. Kathi remembers that after doing very early morning chores, Grandma would have this cake for her along with eggs, bacon, and other breakfast goodies.

1 cup sugar

½ cup cocoa

½ cup shortening

Pinch of salt

2 eggs

½ cup milk

2 teaspoons baking soda

1 teaspoon baking powder

2 cups flour

1 cup hot water

Powdered sugar or frosting

1. Cream together sugar, cocoa, and shortening in medium bowl.
2. Add salt.
3. Beat in eggs and milk.
4. Sift together baking soda, flour, and baking powder.
5. Add hot water to dry ingredients.
6. Add all to cocoa batter.
7. Beat for 2 minutes and pour into a greased and floured 9" × 13" baking dish.
8. Bake at 300° for 30 to 45 minutes.
9. Cool and sprinkle with powdered sugar or a container of prepared frosting.

❧ Serves 15 to 18

And their father Israel said unto them, If it must be so now, do this; take of the best fruits in the land in your vessels, and carry down the man a present, a little balm, and a little honey, spices, and myrrh, nuts, and almonds.

—Genesis 43:11

Wacky Cake

Be sure to follow directions for this wacky cake from my wacky friend, Kathi. I'm just kidding about Kathi, but not about the instructions. Wacky as it is, it works. I like mine iced with chocolate frosting.

1½ cups flour

1 cup sugar

3 tablespoons cocoa

1 teaspoon baking soda

½ teaspoon salt

1 tablespoon vinegar

6 tablespoons vegetable oil

1 teaspoon vanilla

1 cup cold water

Frosting:

¾ to 1 cup sugar

¼ cup butter

½ cup cocoa

⅓ cup cornstarch

¼ teaspoon salt

2 cups milk

1. Sift together flour, sugar, cocoa, baking soda, and salt and put into greased and floured 8" × 8" baking dish.
2. Level off and punch 3 holes into mixture with back of spoon.
3. Pour vinegar into the first hole.
4. Pour vegetable oil into the second hole.
5. Pour vanilla into the third hole.
6. Pour water over all and stir with a fork.
7. Bake at 350° for 25 minutes.
8. Mix together all frosting ingredients and cook until mixture thickens.
9. Spread on top of cooled cake.

Serves 9

If the LORD delight in us, then he will bring us into this land, and give it us; a land which floweth with milk and honey.

—Numbers 14:8

Old-Fashioned Icebox Cake

Buying an already baked angel food cake is what makes this cake so easy. If you want to make this an even richer dessert, serve it with ice cream.

2 envelopes unflavored gelatin

2 cups milk

1 12-ounce package semisweet chocolate chips

1 cup chopped pecans

1 8-ounce container frozen whipped topping, thawed

1 angel food cake, torn into small pieces

1. In medium saucepan, sprinkle unflavored gelatin over 1 cup milk.
2. Let stand 1 minute.
3. Stir over low heat until gelatin is completely dissolved, about 5 minutes.
4. Add chocolate chips and continue cooking, stirring constantly, until chocolate is melted.
5. With wire whisk, beat mixture until chocolate is blended.
6. Stir in remaining milk.
7. Pour into large bowl and chill, stirring occasionally, until mixture mounds slightly when dropped from spoon.
8. Fold in nuts, whipped topping, and cake.
9. Turn into 9" square pan.
10. Chill until set.

Serves 12

Our Favorite Chocolate Cake Roll

When my sister Anita first made this cake roll for her family, she didn't realize it would become the cake of choice for birthdays. I cannot count how many of these she has made for family birthdays—especially since she has five children. It's time consuming, but worth it.

6 egg whites

½ teaspoon cream of tartar

1¼ cups sugar

6 egg yolks

5 tablespoons cocoa

4 tablespoons sifted flour

¼ teaspoon salt

1½ teaspoons vanilla

Confectioners' sugar

Filling:

1 teaspoon unflavored gelatin

2 tablespoons milk

Hot water

2 cups of cold whipping cream

½ cup confectioners' sugar

2 teaspoons vanilla

1 16-ounce can of chocolate frosting topping

1. Beat egg whites and cream of tartar until stiff.
2. Gradually beat in ½ cup sugar until glossy.

continued

(Our Favorite Chocolate Cake Roll—continued)

3. In separate bowl, beat egg yolks until thick and lemon-colored and gradually add ¾ cups sugar.
4. Sift together cocoa, flour, and salt and beat into yolk mixture.
5. Stir in vanilla. Carefully fold into egg white mixture.
6. Spread in shallow 15½" × 10½" pan lined with greased waxed paper.
7. Bake until surface springs back when touched lightly with finger.
8. Immediately turn upside down onto towel sprinkled with confectioners' sugar.
9. Immediately remove paper from cake and roll cake up in sugared towel and cool.
10. While cake is baking, make whipped cream filling. Combine unflavored gelatin and milk in a cup and place in bowl of hot water.
11. Stir until gelatin is dissolved; remove from water and set aside to cool.
12. Whip cold whipping cream until stiff.
13. Beat in confectioners' sugar.
14. Stir in cooled gelatin plus vanilla.
15. Unroll cake roll and spread whipped cream filling over cake roll, leaving about ½ inch edge. Roll cake up, beginning at side and ending with seam side down.
16. Ice with 1 16-ounce can of chocolate frosting. Warm frosting in microwave for 20 seconds to spread more easily.
17. Refrigerate until served.

Serves 12 to 16

Apple Spice Cake

Simple directions for a simple cake. Although Annis didn't frost this cake, I used a vanilla frosting and it was delicious.

1 18.25-ounce box spice cake mix
1 21-ounce can apple pie filling
2 eggs
½ cup oil

1. Put all ingredients in a bowl and mix well.
2. Pour into a greased 9" × 13" baking dish.
3. Bake at 350° for 30 minutes.

Serves 12 to 15

The people asked, and he brought quails, and satisfied them with the bread of heaven.

—Psalms 105:40

Raspberry Cake

You can try this cake substituting strawberries or peaches and it will be just as delicious. I like to garnish it with sliced toasted almonds as well.

1 3-ounce box raspberry gelatin
1 cup boiling water
2 16-ounce packages frozen raspberries
1 angel food cake, already baked
1 12-ounce container frozen whipped topping, thawed
2 tablespoons raspberry preserves

1. Dissolve gelatin in hot water.
2. When dissolved, add 1 package raspberries and mix well.
3. Line bottom of a greased 9" × 13" dish with cake torn into bite-size pieces.
4. Drizzle raspberry gelatin mixture over cake.
5. Mix half of frozen whipped topping with remaining package of raspberries.
6. Spread over cake and gelatin. Top with remaining topping.
7. Refrigerate for 4 to 6 hours.
8. When time to serve, warm 2 tablespoons raspberry preserves in microwave for 10 seconds. Drizzle over topping.

Serves 12 to 15

Pumpkin Pie Cake

No wonder this cake that Sylvia makes is so good—take a look at the amount of butter in it.

4 eggs, slightly beaten
1 16-ounce can pumpkin
1½ cups sugar
2 teaspoons pumpkin pie spice
1 teaspoon salt
1 13-ounce can evaporated milk
1 18.75-ounce box yellow cake mix
2 sticks melted butter
½ cup chopped pecans

1. Mix together eggs, pumpkin, sugar, pumpkin pie spice, salt, and evaporated milk.
2. Pour into a greased and floured 9" × 13" baking dish.
3. Sprinkle cake mix over pumpkin mixture.
4. Pour melted butter over the top of cake.
5. Sprinkle with pecans.
6. Bake at 350° for 1 hour or until toothpick inserted in center comes out clean.

Serves 12 to 15

Anything Goes Cake

As I was finishing my book, my sister-in-law Gayle called and said she had a cake recipe from her long-time friend Barb that was so good and so easy, I just had to include it. Barb has tried this, using all kinds of variations successfully, so you can use any combination you have in your pantry or that sounds appealing to you. Barb's personal favorite is chocolate pudding, chocolate cake mix, and chocolate chips. Sounds great to me.

1 3-ounce package cook-and-serve pudding
1 18.75-ounce package cake mix
   (Barb likes Duncan Hines best)
1 cup chocolate chips
Vegetable cooking spray

1. Cook the pudding according to the directions on the package, being sure to use a large pan.
2. When pudding is finished, stir the cake mix into the pudding, blending well. Sometimes you may have to add a little water if it is too thick. Batter should be like brownie mix.
3. Put into a 9" × 13" baking dish sprayed with vegetable cooking spray. Sprinkle chocolate chips over cake batter.
4. Bake at 350° according to the directions on cake mix package.
5. Remove from oven.
6. Serve warm or cool.

Serves 12 to 15

Three-Layer Dessert Bar

These dessert bars are deliciously grand, and terribly easy to make and take. Everyone will rave about them.

First Layer:
5 tablespoons sugar
¼ cup cocoa
1 egg, beaten
½ cup melted butter
1 teaspoon vanilla
2 cups crushed graham crackers
1 cup fine coconut
½ cup nuts

Second Layer:
3 tablespoons milk
2 tablespoons vanilla instant pudding
¼ cup butter melted
2 cups powdered sugar

Third Layer:
4 squares semisweet chocolate
1 tablespoon butter or margarine

1. For first layer, mix together all ingredients and press into greased 11" × 15" jelly roll pan and chill for 1 hour.

continued

2. For second layer, combine all ingredients and beat with electric beater for 2 minutes. Spread on top of first layer and then chill for 1 to 2 hours.
3. Melt chocolate and butter together in microwave for 1 minute.
4. Remove and stir. Microwave for 30 seconds more if necessary.
5. Spread on top of third layer.
6. Refrigerate for 3 to 4 hours or overnight.

Makes 36

Butter of kine, and milk of sheep,
with fat of lambs, and rams of the breed
of Bashan, and goats, with the fat of
kidneys of wheat; and thou didst
drink the pure blood of the grape.

—Deuteronomy 32:14

Cherry Almond Treats

My good friend Vicki always brings us a wonderful tray of goodies at Christmas. This is one of my favorites that she shared with me.

1 cup margarine or butter

½ cup sugar

1 egg yolk

½ teaspoon salt

2½ cups flour

4 egg whites at room temperature

¼ teaspoon cream of tartar

10 tablespoons sugar

¾ cup ground almonds

1 cup cherry preserves

1. Cream together margarine and sugar.
2. Stir in egg yolk.
3. Add salt and flour to creamed mixture.
4. Put dough mixture into 15" × 10" × 1" greased baking dish.
5. Bake for 20 minutes.
6. Beat egg whites until stiff, adding in cream of tartar.
7. Gradually beat in sugar with egg whites.
8. Combine almonds with cherry preserves and spread over dough.
9. Spread egg white mixture on top of preserves.
10. Bake 10 to 15 minutes or until lightly browned.
11. Cut when cool.

Makes 24

Caramel Turtle Brownies

This is one of the few recipes that my microwave-cooking friend Kathi doesn't fix in the microwave. This is such a popular recipe that I'm sure you've had it at many of your church carry-ins.

1 18.25-ounce package German chocolate cake mix
¾ cup melted butter
⅔ cup evaporated milk
14 ounces Kraft caramels
1 cup of chocolate chips
½ cup pecan pieces

1. Mix together cake mix, melted butter, and ⅓ cup of the evaporated milk. Put half of this mixture in greased 9" × 13" baking dish. Bake 6 minutes.
2. Melt caramels with remaining ⅓ cup evaporated milk on low heat, stirring while melting.
3. While cake is still hot, pour caramel mixture on top of cake. Sprinkle chocolate chips over caramel and then top with nuts.
4. Spread remaining cake mixture on top of nuts.
5. Bake at 350° for 20 to 25 minutes.
6. If desired, frost with chocolate icing.

Makes 24 pieces

Date Pinwheels

My sister Lois shared this recipe with me as she has shared it with so many others over the years. Take these pinwheels with you, and you'll be sharing as well.

1 pound of pitted dates, chopped
½ cup water
½ cup granulated sugar
½ cup butter
½ cup brown sugar
½ cup granulated sugar
1 egg, well beaten
½ teaspoon vanilla
2 cups sifted flour
½ teaspoon baking soda
1½ cups chopped pecans

1. Combine dates, water, and ½ cup granulated sugar.
2. Cook until thick (2 to 3 minutes), stirring constantly. Cool.
3. Cream together butter and sugars. Add egg and vanilla and beat well.
4. Sift dry ingredients and add to creamed butter mixture.
5. Stir until smooth. Chill while making the date mixture.

continued

(Date Pinwheels—continued)

6. Divide dough in half. Roll one part on lightly floured surface till ¼" thick.
7. Combine date mixture and nuts.
8. Spread half of filling evenly over dough.
9. Roll like a jelly roll.
10. Wrap in waxed paper with open edge of roll on bottom.
11. Repeat with remaining dough and filling. Chill rolls till firm.
12. Cut in ¼" slices.
13. Place on lightly greased baking sheet.
14. Bake at 400° for 8 to 10 minutes.

Makes about 3 dozen

Hast thou not poured me out as milk,
and curdled me like cheese?

—Job 10:10

Oatmeal Carmelitas

I received this recipe back in 1977 when my husband's boss's wife, Lois, brought it to one of our first office parties in Dayton. When I make these, I remember this lovely lady who all of us were so fond of.

1 cup flour

1 cup quick-cooking oats

½ teaspoon baking soda

¼ teaspoon salt

½ cup packed light brown sugar

¾ cup butter or margarine, melted

1 6-ounce package chocolate chips

½ cup chopped nuts

¾ cup caramel ice cream topping

3 tablespoons flour

1. Preheat oven to 350°.
2. Grease bottom and sides of 9" square baking dish.
3. Combine flour, oats, baking soda, salt, brown sugar, and margarine in large bowl and mix to form crumbs.
4. Press half of mixture into bottom of greased 9" square baking dish.
5. Bake at 350° for 10 minutes.
6. Remove from oven and sprinkle chocolate and nuts over crumb mixture.

continued

7. Microwave caramel topping for 10 to 20 seconds. Mix caramel topping and flour together well. Drizzle over chocolate and nuts.
8. Sprinkle remaining crumbs over caramel topping.
9. Bake at 350° for 15 to 20 minutes until golden brown.
10. Chill bars for easy cutting.

Makes 9 to 12 bars

And he said unto her, Give me, I pray thee, a little water to drink; for I am thirsty. And she opened a bottle of milk, and gave him drink, and covered him.

—*Judges 4:19*

Peanut Butter Squares

When Pat brought these to one of our annual office picnics, we all wanted this yummy recipe. Few things are better than peanut butter and chocolate!

½ cup light corn syrup
½ cup brown sugar
1 cup peanut butter
2 cups Rice Krispies
¼ cup butter or margarine, melted
2 tablespoons vanilla
2 tablespoons milk
2 cups confectioners' sugar
1 3-ounce package of instant vanilla pudding (not sugar-free)
¼ cup butter or margarine
1 cup chocolate chips

1. In saucepan over medium low heat, combine corn syrup, brown sugar, and peanut butter until peanut butter is melted.
2. Remove from heat and add Rice Krispies. Press into a 9" × 13" baking dish.
3. Refrigerate while making the middle layer.
4. In bowl, combine melted butter with vanilla, milk, sugar, and instant pudding.
5. Spread evenly over the base layer.
6. Refrigerate for 15 minutes or until firm.
7. In a saucepan over medium heat, melt margarine and chocolate chips and mix together.

continued

(Peanut Butter Squares—continued)

8. Spread evenly over middle layer.
9. Refrigerate until chocolate layer is firm.
10. Set the cookies out for about 10 minutes before cutting. Cut into 48 pieces. These cookies do not have to be stored in the refrigerator.

Makes 48 small pieces

And he gathered up all the food of the seven years, which were in the land of Egypt, and laid up the food in the cities: the food of the field, which was round about every city, laid he up in the same.

—*Genesis 41:48*

Pecan Puffs

My sister Marilyn forms these into rolls and chills them. Then she slices them and they become Mexican wedding cookies. And she carries them wherever she goes.

4 tablespoons powdered sugar
½ cup shortening
1 tablespoon water
2 teaspoons vanilla
2 cups flour
1 cup pecan pieces
Powdered sugar

1. Cream together sugar and shortening.
2. Mix in water and vanilla.
3. Add flour and nuts; chill.
4. Form into small balls and bake at 250° for 40 to 50 minutes.
5. Remove from oven and roll twice in powdered sugar.

Makes 3 dozen

Toffee Bars

One of my favorite candy bars is Hershey's Symphony bar. These Toffee Bars could be called candy bars and they satisfy almost anyone's sweet tooth. A good treat to take along anytime.

2 cups firmly packed brown sugar

2 cups flour

½ cup butter or margarine, softened

1 teaspoon baking powder

½ teaspoon salt

1 teaspoon vanilla extract

1 cup milk

1 egg

½ cup semisweet chocolate chips

1 cup Symphony candy bar, broken into pieces

½ cup chopped unblanched almonds

1. Preheat oven to 350°. Grease a 9" × 13" baking dish.
2. In a large mixing bowl, mix together brown sugar and flour.
3. Using a pastry cutter or two knives, cut in the butter until mixture resembles crumbs. Remove 1 cup of mixture and set aside.
4. To mixture in large bowl, add baking powder and salt. Using a whisk, lightly beat in vanilla, milk, and egg.
5. Continue beating until a smooth batter forms. Pour batter into prepared baking dish.
6. Sprinkle reserved crumb mixture over top of batter in pan. Sprinkle with the chocolate chips, broken candy bar pieces, and almonds.
7. Bake bars for 35 minutes, or until a toothpick inserted in center comes out clean.
8. Cool bars before cutting.

Makes 24 bars

And take with thee ten loaves, and cracknels, and a cruse of honey, and go to him: he shall tell thee what shall become of the child.

—1 Kings 14:3

S'Mores

It's true that everyone always wants some more of these delectable chocolate marshmallowy treats. It happens when they're brought in for any occasion.

8 to 10 whole graham crackers
1 19.8-ounce package fudge brownie mix
2 cups miniature marshmallows
1 cup milk chocolate chips
½ cup chopped peanuts

1. Arrange graham crackers in a single layer in a greased 9" × 13" baking dish.
2. Prepare the brownie batter according to package directions.
3. Spread over crackers.
4. Bake at 350° for 25 to 30 minutes or until a toothpick inserted near the center comes out clean.
5. Sprinkle with marshmallows, chocolate chips, and peanuts.
6. Bake 5 minutes longer or until marshmallows are slightly puffed and golden brown.
7. Cool before cutting.

Makes 2 dozen

Cream Cheese Finger Cookies

This is one of the many recipes that Annis has shared with me along with the beautiful poems she has written. These are great to take to a Christmas cookie exchange.

½ cup butter (no substitutes), softened
4 ounces cream cheese, softened
1 teaspoon vanilla extract
1¾ cups flour
1 tablespoon powdered sugar
Dash salt
1 cup finely chopped pecans
Powdered sugar

1. In a mixing bowl, cream together butter and cream cheese.
2. Beat in vanilla.
3. Combine the flour, sugar, and salt and gradually add to cream cheese mixture.
4. Stir in pecans; dough will be crumbly.
5. Shape tablespoonfuls into 2" logs.
6. Place 2" apart on ungreased cookie sheets.
7. Bake at 375° for 12 to 14 minutes or until lightly browned.
8. Roll warm cookies in powdered sugar.

Makes 2 dozen

Double Chocolate Chip Cookies

You'll find that adults as well as children will love these cookies that Annis gave me. You may want to make two batches to take.

1 18.25-ounce box devil's food cake mix

1 stick butter

1 teaspoon vanilla

2 eggs

½ cup chopped pecans

1 cup semisweet chocolate chips

1 package mini M&Ms

Walnut pieces

1. Heat oven to 375°.
2. In a large bowl, using a mixer, beat half the dry cake mix with the butter, vanilla, and eggs.
3. Beat in remaining cake mix. Stir in nuts and chocolate chips.
4. Drop dough by rounded teaspoonfuls or use a small cookie scoop.
5. Top with a few mini M&Ms and walnut pieces.
6. Bake for 10 to 12 minutes on ungreased cookie sheets.
7. Bake until edges are set. Centers will be soft.
8. Cool on wire rack for 1 minute before removing from cookie sheet.

Makes 5 dozen

White Chocolate Oatmeal Cookies

Welcome a neighbor with these wonderful white chocolate oatmeal cookies. The white chocolate and oatmeal combination is sure to satisfy anyone's taste buds. My friend Annis's neighbor Madolin passed this recipe on to her, and she in turn has passed it on to me.

2 sticks butter

1 cup sugar

1 cup brown sugar

2 large eggs

2 teaspoons vanilla

3 cups flour

1 teaspoon baking soda

1 teaspoon baking powder

1 teaspoon salt

1½ cups regular Old-Fashioned oats

2 cups white chocolate chips

1. Cream together butter, sugars, and eggs.
2. Beat and add vanilla.
3. Mix together dry ingredients.
4. Mix with creamed mixture.
5. Add white chocolate chips.
6. Bake at 350° for 8 to 10 minutes.
7. Cool for 2 minutes before removing from cookie sheet.

Makes 3 dozen

Fruit and Nut Bars

Annis tells me that these California fruit bars her friend Anna makes are so delicious that they're gone almost as soon as they're served.

½ cup white flour

1 cup oats

¾ cup firmly packed brown sugar

¼ cup whole wheat flour

1 stick butter, softened

2 teaspoons vanilla

1½ cups chopped walnuts

1 cup golden raisins

1 cup chopped dried apricots

1 14-ounce can sweetened condensed milk

1. Preheat oven to 350°.
2. In a large bowl, combine flour, oats, sugar, wheat flour, butter, and vanilla.
3. Mix until crumbly.
4. Reserve ½ cup of crumb mixture and set aside.
5. Press remainder on bottom of greased 9" × 13" baking dish.
6. In a large bowl, combine walnuts, raisins, apricots, and milk.
7. Spoon evenly over crust.
8. Top with reserved crumb mixture and press down firmly.
9. Bake for 25 minutes or until edges are lightly browned.
10. Cool before cutting into bars.
11. Can be stored covered at room temperature for 3 to 4 days.

Makes 32

I have fed you with milk, and not with meat: for hitherto ye were not able to bear it, neither yet now are ye able.

—1 Corinthians 3:2

Pecan Bars

Annis has been a wonderful source for the delectable recipes included in this cookbook. She has another knockout with these yummy pecan bars.

Crust:
3 cups flour
½ cup sugar
1 cup butter
Dash salt

Filling:
4 eggs
1½ cups dark Karo syrup
1½ cups sugar
3 tablespoons butter, softened
1½ teaspoons vanilla
1½ cups roasted salted pecans

1. For crust, mix together flour, sugar, butter, and salt. Press mixture into a greased and floured 9" × 13" baking dish.
2. Bake at 350° for 20 minutes.
3. For filling, combine eggs, dark Karo syrup, sugar, butter, vanilla, and pecans.
4. Pour on crust.
5. Bake at 350° for 25 minutes.

⁂ Makes 24

Chocolate-Raspberry Brownies

Who doesn't like chocolate and raspberry together? It's one of my personal favorite combinations. This would also be good with white chocolate chips in place of the milk chocolate chips.

1 18.25-ounce package devil's food cake mix
¾ cup melted butter
1 cup chopped nuts
⅓ cup evaporated milk
Vegetable cooking spray
1 cup milk chocolate chips
1 16-ounce bag of frozen raspberries, thawed

1. Preheat oven to 350°.
2. Combine cake mix, melted butter, nuts, and evaporated milk, and stir by hand until dough holds together.
3. Press half of dough into 9" × 13" baking dish coated with vegetable spray and bake for 6 minutes to make crust.
4. Sprinkle chocolate chips over baked crust.
5. Place raspberries over chocolate chips.
6. Crumble remaining dough over raspberries.
7. Bake for 15 to 18 minutes.
8. Cool and refrigerate for 30 minutes.
9. Cut into squares.

⁂ Makes 24

Fresh Apple Cookies

The glaze used on these cookies makes this recipe stand out. Try them for your next carry-in, and they'll stand out there as well. Dig in!

½ cup vegetable shortening

1⅓ cups firmly packed brown sugar

½ teaspoon salt

1 teaspoon cinnamon

1 teaspoon nutmeg

1 egg

2 cups flour

1 teaspoon baking soda

¼ cup milk

4 peeled, cored, and finely chopped apples

1 cup chopped walnuts

Vegetable cooking spray

Vanilla Glaze:

1½ cups powdered sugar

1 tablespoon butter, melted

⅛ teaspoon salt

3 tablespoons milk

½ teaspoon vanilla

Nonstick vegetable cooking spray

1. Preheat oven to 400°.
2. In a large bowl, cream the shortening, brown sugar, salt, cinnamon, nutmeg, and egg.
3. Add the flour and baking soda and mix well.
4. Stir in the milk until well blended.
5. Stir in the apples and walnuts.
6. Drop by teaspoonfuls onto cookie sheets that have been coated with vegetable cooking spray.
7. Bake 11 to 14 minutes or until golden brown.
8. While cookies are baking, in a small bowl combine all glaze ingredients and mix until smooth.
9. Remove cookies from cookie sheets and, while still hot, spread on vanilla glaze.

✦ Makes 4 dozen

And kept the feast of unleavened bread seven days with joy: for the LORD had made them joyful, and turned the heart of the king of Assyria unto them, to strengthen their hands in the work of the house of God, the God of Israel.

—Ezra 6:22

Almond Glaze Sugar Cookies

I fell in love with these cookies the first time I tried them. This is another wonderful recipe that Laura got from our friend Carolyn and passed on to me for this book.

1 cup Land O'Lakes soft baking butter with canola oil
¾ cup sugar
1 teaspoon almond extract
2 cups flour
½ teaspoon baking powder
Granulated sugar

Glaze:
1½ cups powdered sugar
1 teaspoon almond extract
4 to 5 teaspoons water
Sliced almonds

1. Heat oven to 400°.
2. In a large mixing bowl, combine butter, sugar, almond extract, flour, and baking powder.
3. Beat at medium speed until creamy.
4. Drop dough by rounded spoonfuls onto greased cookie sheets.
5. Flatten to ¼" thickness with bottom of buttered glass dipped in granulated sugar.
6. Bake 7 to 9 minutes or until edges are very lightly browned.
7. Cool 1 minute and remove from cookie sheets to cool completely.
8. Stir together all glaze ingredients except almonds with wire whisk in a small bowl.
9. Decorate cooled cookies with glaze and almonds as desired.

 Makes 3 dozen

And it shall come to pass in the increase, that ye shall give the fifth part unto Pharaoh, and four parts shall be your own, for seed of the field, and for your food, and for them of your households, and for food for your little ones.

—Genesis 47:24

Forgotten Meringues

This recipe is from Laura's daughter, Ann. Meringues are one of my favorite type of cookies and very easy to make. Eating them is like putting sugar in your mouth.

2 egg whites
Pinch of salt
2/3 cup sugar
1 teaspoon vanilla
1 cup mini semisweet chocolate morsels

1. Beat egg whites until foamy.
2. Add salt and continue beating until whites stand in soft peaks.
3. Gradually add the sugar, beating until very stiff peaks form.
4. Sprinkle in vanilla and chocolate morsels on top.
5. Fold in.
6. Preheat oven to 350°.
7. Drop by teaspoon onto lightly buttered cookie sheets. They may be placed close together—they will not spread.
8. Place in the heated oven and immediately turn it off.
9. Let the cookies dry overnight in the cooling oven.

🦢 Makes 24

Loaded Cookies

I call these cookies "loaded" because they are loaded with so many good things—a mouthful of tasty treats all rolled into one cookie.

½ cup butter
½ teaspoon vanilla
1 egg
¼ cup sugar
½ cup packed brown sugar
1½ cups flour
¾ teaspoon baking soda
¼ teaspoon baking powder
½ cup chocolate M&Ms
½ cup rolled oats
½ cup crisped rice cereal
½ cup white chocolate chips
½ cup chocolate chips

1. In a large bowl, cream together butter, vanilla, and egg.
2. Add remaining ingredients and stir until well blended.
3. Place teaspoon-size dough balls onto an ungreased cookie sheet.
4. Bake at 350° for 10 to 12 minutes until lightly browned.

🦢 Makes 4 dozen

Mounds Cookies

If you're a coconut lover, you're sure to love these Mounds cookies Ellen passed along to me via Kathi. With the addition of almonds to this recipe, it's like an Almond Joy and Mounds rolled into one. "Sometimes you feel like a nut, sometimes you don't."

1¼ cups flour

½ teaspoon baking soda

½ teaspoon salt

½ cup margarine, softened

¾ cup sugar

1 egg

1 cup Mounds candy bars broken into small pieces, approximately 2 bars

½ teaspoon vanilla

½ cup chopped roasted almonds

1. In medium bowl, sift together flour, baking soda, and salt.
2. Cream margarine and sugar in separate bowl.
3. Beat in egg.
4. Add flour mixture to creamed butter mixture and add candy bars and almonds.
5. Stir in vanilla.
6. Refrigerate dough for 30 minutes.
7. Drop by half-teaspoonfuls onto greased cookie sheet.
8. Bake at 350° for 10 to 12 minutes.

Makes 3 dozen

Crisp Oatmeal Cookies

Judee's oatmeal cookies have been a tradition in her family for many years. I was pleased that she was willing to share this old-fashioned cookie recipe with me.

6 tablespoons milk

1 teaspoon vinegar or lemon juice

¾ cup light brown sugar

¾ cup dark brown sugar

¾ cup vegetable oil

½ teaspoon salt

¾ teaspoon baking soda

¾ teaspoon vanilla

1½ cups flour

3 cups quick oats

¾ cup finely chopped walnuts

1. Combine milk and vinegar in bowl and let stand 10 minutes.
2. In large bowl, combine all the remaining ingredients in the order given.
3. After 10 minutes, stir in milk mixture. You may want to use an electric mixer to mix dough.
4. Roll into balls the size of walnuts, or larger if you like big cookies.
5. Place on cookie sheet and flatten to ⅛" with a fork dipped in milk.

continued

6. Bake at 375° for 8 to 10 minutes.
7. Leave on pan for 2 to 3 minutes before removing from pan.

Makes 3 dozen

And the priest shall burn it upon the altar: it is the food of the offering made by fire unto the LORD.

—Leviticus 3:11

Deliciously Easy Brownies

My friend Vicki first gave me this recipe in 1985 when I had my confectionary retail store. They were one of the most popular items we sold. They can be made with or without the white chocolate glaze—they're delicious either way.

1 19.8-ounce box of fudge brownies
¼ cup water
½ cup vegetable oil
2 eggs
3 tablespoons margarine, softened
½ cup packed brown sugar
½ cup pecan pieces
½ cup white chocolate chips
1 teaspoon milk

1. In medium bowl, combine brownie mix, water, oil, and eggs until well blended.
2. In small bowl, combine margarine and brown sugar, creaming together.
3. Mix pecans into brown sugar mixture.
4. Spread brownie batter into greased 9" × 13" baking dish.
5. Distribute nut mixture evenly over the brownie batter.
6. Bake at 350° for 28 to 30 minutes.
7. While they are cooling, melt the chocolate chips in a microwaveable bowl for 1 minute.

continued

8. Remove and stir.
9. Place in microwave again for 15 to 30 seconds and remove.
10. Stir until melted.
11. With whisk, combine milk with white chocolate.
12. Drizzle over brownies
13. Cool.

Makes 24

Behold, therefore I will deliver thee to the men of the east for a possession, and they shall set their palaces in thee, and make their dwellings in thee: they shall eat thy fruit, and they shall drink thy milk.

—Ezekiel 25:4

Chocolate Cream Cheese Brownies

My sister-in-law Gayle started one of our Christmas family traditions when she brought these to our home about ten years ago. She has brought them every year since, and we all eagerly wait for them—and her—to arrive.

Bar:

1 19.8-ounce box of fudge brownie mix

¼ cup water

½ cup vegetable oil

2 eggs

Filling:

1 8-ounce package of cream cheese, reserving 2 ounces, softened

½ cup sugar

1 egg

2 tablespoons flour

½ teaspoon vanilla

¼ cup margarine

½ cup chopped pecans

2 cups chocolate chips

Frosting:

¼ cup margarine

1 square unsweetened chocolate

2 ounces cream cheese (reserved from above)

1 teaspoon vanilla

¼ cup milk

1 pound powdered sugar

continued

(Chocolate Cream Cheese Brownies—continued)

1. In medium bowl, combine brownie mix, water, oil, and 2 eggs until well blended, then pour into a greased and floured 9" × 13" baking dish.
2. Mix together 6 ounces cream cheese, ½ cup sugar, 1 egg, flour, ½ teaspoon vanilla, ¼ cup margarine, and pecans and spread over bar mixture.
3. Top with chocolate chips.
4. Bake at 350° for 25 to 35 minutes.
5. Mix together ¼ cup margarine, unsweetened chocolate, 2 ounces cream cheese, 1 teaspoon vanilla, milk, and powdered sugar. Spread on top of brownies. Refrigerate when cool.

✥ Makes 24 to 36

Come, eat of my bread, and drink of the wine which I have mingled.

—Proverbs 9:5

Snowy Nutballs

These little confections are full of nuts and flavor. They are dusted with lots of powdered sugar, so make sure to serve napkins with them. They're finger-licking good.

1 cup butter or margarine

½ cup powdered sugar

1 teaspoon vanilla

2¼ cups flour

¼ teaspoon salt

¾ cup finely chopped nuts

1. Preheat oven to 400°.
2. In medium bowl, combine all ingredients.
3. Drop in small spoonfuls onto ungreased cookie sheet.
4. Bake 10 to 12 minutes.
5. While warm, roll in powdered sugar.
6. Cool and roll in powdered sugar again.

✥ Makes 3 dozen

Chocolate Peanut Brownies

Snickers are a favorite in our family, so these brownies that remind us of them were a big hit with everyone. This is a great dessert to take along to a family gathering. Enjoy.

1 14-ounce package of caramels

¾ cup condensed milk

1 18.25-ounce package of German Chocolate cake mix

1 cup chopped peanuts

¾ cup melted butter

1 6-ounce package chocolate chips

1. Melt caramels and ⅓ cup of milk in pan over hot water and set aside, keeping warm.
2. Combine cake mix, peanuts, butter, chocolate chips, and remaining milk and stir until crumbly.
3. Press half of mixture in a greased and floured 9" × 13" baking dish.
4. Bake at 350° for 6 minutes.
5. Remove and cool slightly.
6. Sprinkle chips over dough.
7. Quickly spread caramel mixture on top.
8. Spread remaining crumbs.
9. Press lightly with spoon.
10. Return to oven at 350° for 14 to 18 minutes.
11. Cool 30 minutes and refrigerate until firm and set.

Makes 24

Ritz Supreme Dessert

My sister Marilyn is very picky about what she eats and loves to eat desserts and chocolate candy. I don't know how she has stayed so trim all these years. This recipe of hers will satisfy anyone's sweet tooth.

3 egg whites

1 cup sugar

1 teaspoon baking powder

20 Ritz crackers, crushed fine

¾ cup chopped pecans

1 8-ounce container frozen whipped topping, thawed

Hot fudge sauce

1. Beat egg whites until stiff.
2. Add sugar gradually, and fold in baking powder.
3. Continue beating until batter forms stiff peaks.
4. Fold in cracker crumbs and pecans.
5. Pour into a greased 9" pie pan and bake at 350° for 25 minutes.
6. Cool.
7. Top with whipped topping and drizzle with hot fudge sauce when ready to serve.

Serves 8

Bananas Royale

Annis gets her recipes from many different people. The man who came to install her awning shared this recipe with her, which he and his mom received when their neighbors brought this dish after his father had passed away.

1 cup sour cream
1 12-ounce container frozen whipped topping, thawed
2 cups milk
2 3.4-ounce packages instant vanilla pudding mix
1 11-ounce box of vanilla wafers
5 to 6 large bananas

1. In a large bowl, mix sour cream and whipped topping. Add milk.
2. Stir in both puddings and beat with electric mixer for 2 to 3 minutes.
3. In a greased and floured 9" × 13" baking dish, place a layer of vanilla wafers on the bottom.
4. Cut up bananas and place half of bananas on top of wafers.
5. Place a thin layer of pudding mixture over the bananas.
6. Repeat layers and end with pudding mixture.
7. Crush some of the vanilla wafers in a plastic bag and sprinkle over the top.

🍵 Serves 18 to 20

John Mike Dessert

When Kathi was living in the Washington, D.C. area about 25 years ago, her neighbor made this dessert for her son. It became his favorite recipe, so she named it after him. His name was John Michael.

55 Ritz crackers, crumbled
1 stick margarine, melted
1¼ cups powdered sugar
2 packages Dream Whip whipped topping mix
1 6-ounce can pink lemonade
1 cup sweetened condensed milk

1. Mix crackers, margarine, and sugar. Reserve ⅛ cup of mixture for topping.
2. Place in greased and floured 9" × 13" dish.
3. Prepare Dream Whip according to directions on package.
4. Mix together lemonade and milk.
5. Fold lemonade mixture into Dream Whip.
6. Put on top of cracker mixture.
7. Sprinkle with reserved topping.
8. Refrigerate for at least 6 hours.

🍵 Serves 12 to 15

Dessert Pralines

My sister Marilyn always has sweets on hand in her home. She loves pecans, and this is one of her favorite recipes.

24 graham crackers
2 sticks margarine
1 cup brown sugar
1 cup pecans

1. Place graham crackers on a cookie sheet.
2. In a saucepan, melt margarine and brown sugar. Boil for 1½ minutes.
3. Remove from heat and add pecans.
4. Pour on top of crackers.
5. Bake at 350° for 15 minutes.
6. Cut immediately.

Makes 24

Go thy way, eat thy bread with joy,
and drink thy wine with a merry heart;
for God now accepteth thy works.

—*Ecclesiastes 9:7*

Easy Éclairs

Easy, yummy, and fabulous. The already prepared icing works like a dream with this dessert and makes it a snap to prepare.

3 cups milk
2 3-ounce packages instant French vanilla pudding
1 8-ounce container frozen whipped topping, thawed
1 16-ounce box graham crackers
1 16-ounce container chocolate icing
½ cup roasted and salted chopped peanuts

1. In large bowl, combine milk with both puddings and beat with electric mixer for 2 minutes.
2. Fold in whipped topping.
3. In bottom of greased 9" × 13" dish, place a layer of whole graham crackers.
4. Place entire pudding mixture on top of the graham crackers.
5. Place another layer of graham crackers on top of pudding mixture.
6. Frost graham crackers with canned chocolate icing and sprinkle with nuts.
7. Refrigerate overnight.
8. Cut into squares.

Makes 20 to 24

Angel Squares

My friends Nanette and Nancy shared this recipe with me. They call them angel squares. A fitting name, as I consider Nanette and Nancy friends sent from heaven.

1 cup butter or margarine

2 cups brown sugar

1 teaspoon baking soda

1 cup hot water

2 eggs

3 cups flour

1 teaspoon cinnamon

1 teaspoon baking powder

3 cups chocolate chips

Icing:

4 cups powdered sugar

1/3 cup milk

1/2 teaspoon vanilla

1. Cream butter and sugar.
2. Dissolve baking soda in hot water. Mix in all remaining ingredients except chocolate chips with the butter mixture.
3. Mix well.
4. Stir in chocolate chips.
5. In a greased 11" × 17" cookie sheet with sides, bake at 350° for 20 minutes.
6. For icing, mix powdered sugar, milk, and vanilla until smooth and thin.
7. Top with icing while warm.

🐸 Makes 36

And Melchizedek king of Salem brought forth bread and wine: and he was the priest of the most high God.

—Genesis 14:18

Butter Pecan Bars

Mix it up and drizzle these pecan bars with melted chocolate chips, white or milk chocolate. Either way, they'll be delicious.

2 eggs
1 cup brown sugar
1 cup sugar
1¼ cups flour
¾ cup stick butter, melted
1 teaspoon vanilla
1 cup chopped pecans
Vegetable cooking spray

1. Beat eggs for 1 minute.
2. Add sugars and flour and mix together.
3. Add melted butter, vanilla, and pecans.
4. Spray a 9" × 13" baking dish with vegetable cooking spray and pour batter into pan.
5. Bake at 350° for 35 minutes.
6. Cut into squares while still warm.
7. Store in a tightly sealed container.

 Makes 24

Peachy Pizza

If fresh peaches are available, they can be substituted for the frozen peaches. Be sure to serve this with whipped cream.

1 refrigerated pie crust, at room temperature for 5 to 10 minutes
1 16-ounce bag of frozen peaches, thawed
1 teaspoon cinnamon
½ cup sugar
¼ teaspoon nutmeg
¾ cup flour
½ cup sugar
½ cup butter
½ cup pecans

1. Unfold pie crust and place in greased pizza pan.
2. Cut up peaches into small pieces and put on top of pie crust.
3. Mix together cinnamon, sugar, and nutmeg and put on top of peaches.
4. Mix together flour, sugar, butter, and pecans and put on top of peaches.
5. Bake at 425° for 20 to 25 minutes.

Makes 20 pieces

Frosted Strawberry Squares

This is especially good during the summertime, but it's a welcome treat any time of the year.

1 cup flour
¼ cup brown sugar
⅓ cup chopped pecans
½ cup butter, melted
2 egg whites
2 tablespoons lemon juice
⅔ to 1 cup sugar
1 10-ounce package of frozen strawberries, thawed
1 cup whipped cream

1. Mix flour, brown sugar, pecans, and butter until crumbly.
2. Place in baking dish.
3. Bake for 20 minutes at 350°, stirring occasionally.
4. Remove from oven.
5. Let cool.
6. Beat egg whites, lemon juice, sugar, and strawberries with mixer until standing in peaks.
7. Fold in whipped cream.
8. Pour over crumb mixture.
9. Place remaining crumbs on top.
10. Place in freezer for 6 hours or overnight.

 Makes 12

Date Pudding

The brown sugar sauce really complements this recipe. I'm not a big date lover, but I do like this recipe that my sister Lois has shared with me.

1 cup pitted dates
1 cup boiling water
½ cup sugar
½ cup brown sugar
1 egg
2 tablespoons melted butter
1½ cups flour
1 teaspoon baking soda
½ teaspoon baking powder
½ teaspoon salt
1 cup chopped walnuts

Brown Sugar Sauce:
1½ cups brown sugar
1 tablespoon butter
½ cup boiling water

1. Combine dates and water.
2. In large bowl blend sugars, egg, and butter.
3. In medium bowl, sift together dry ingredients; add to sugar mixture.
4. Stir walnuts and cooked date mixture into sugar mixture.

continued

(Date Pudding—continued)

5. Pour into greased 8" × 8" baking dish.
6. Combine brown sugar, butter, and boiling water.
7. Whisk together and pour over date pudding.
   Bake in oven at 375° for 40 minutes.

🐛 Serves 9 to 12

Then answered one of the people, and said,
Thy father straitly charged the people with an
oath, saying, Cursed be the man that eateth
any food this day. And the people were faint.

—1 Samuel 14:28

Butterscotch Dessert

Get out the ice cream and whip up a treat! This scrumptious dessert will be welcome for any occasion.

30 Ritz crackers, crushed
1 1/3 cups margarine, melted
Vegetable cooking spray
1 12-ounce jar hot fudge topping
6 to 8 Heath bars, crushed
1 quart vanilla ice cream
2 3-ounce packages instant butterscotch pudding
1 cup milk
1 12-ounce container frozen whipped topping, thawed

1. Mix together crackers and margarine.
2. Spray 9" × 13" dish with vegetable cooking spray and press cracker mixture on bottom.
3. Warm hot fudge sauce in microwave for 10 to 12 seconds so it will spread more easily.
4. Spread fudge sauce over cracker crust.
5. Sprinkle crushed Heath bars onto fudge topping.
6. Beat together ice cream, pudding, and milk for 2 minutes with electric mixer.
7. Pour over cracker crust and refrigerate for 4 to 6 hours.
8. Top with whipped topping.

🐛 Serves 15

Kathi's Bread Pudding

This hand-me-down recipe is an old-fashioned one passed down in Kathi's family for many generations. Her mom always made it with leftover bread, and she has graciously shared it with all of us. The sauce really makes this recipe—it's delightful.

2 cups dry bread crumbs

2 cups scalded milk

6 tablespoons sugar

Pinch salt

2 eggs, slightly beaten

2 tablespoons butter, softened

½ teaspoon vanilla

1 cup raisins

Whipped cream

Vanilla Sauce:

1 cup water

½ cup sugar

2 tablespoons cornstarch

2 tablespoons butter

1 teaspoon vanilla

Whipped cream

1. Put bread crumbs into greased 8" x 8" greased baking dish. Pour 1 cup scalded milk over bread crumbs and soak for 30 minutes.

2. Mix together sugar, salt, eggs, and 1 cup scalded milk.
3. Add butter, vanilla, and raisins.
4. Pour mixture over soaked bread crumbs and bake for 40 minutes at 350°.
5. For vanilla sauce, cook water, sugar, and cornstarch until thick.
6. Remove from heat and add butter and vanilla. Whisk together.
7. Serve with whipped cream.

 Serves 9

And he pressed upon them greatly; and they turned in unto him, and entered into his house; and he made them a feast, and did bake unleavened bread, and they did eat.

—Genesis 19:3

Fruit Salad

You can whip this dessert up in five minutes, and it will be ready to serve in less than an hour. Add a teaspoon of almond flavoring and it will be irresistible.

1 3.4-ounce box vanilla instant pudding
1 3.3-ounce box white chocolate instant pudding
1 20-ounce can pineapple, crushed, not drained
1 20-ounce can pineapple chunks, not drained
1 29-ounce can fruit cocktail, drained
1 15-ounce can mandarin oranges, drained
2 8-ounce containers frozen whipped topping, thawed
1 cup pecan pieces

1. Mix puddings and pineapple.
2. Refrigerate for 30 to 40 minutes.
3. Add remaining ingredients.
4. Refrigerate until ready to serve.

 Serves 10 to 12

PB and Chocolate Squares

For all you peanut-butter-and-chocolate lovers, this is one easy snack to make. Cut the squares smaller so everyone gets a piece. This one will be gone quickly.

2½ cups chunky peanut butter
2 sticks margarine, melted
5 cups powdered sugar
3 cups Rice Krispies
Vegetable cooking spray
1½ cups chocolate chips
6 tablespoons margarine, melted

1. In microwaveable bowl, soften peanut butter in microwave for only 15 seconds.
2. Combine with margarine until well blended.
3. In large bowl, combine powdered sugar with peanut butter mixture. Mix in Rice Krispies.
4. Spray 9" × 13" dish with vegetable cooking spray.
5. Spread and press peanut butter mixture into pan.
6. Combine chocolate chips and margarine. If necessary, put in microwave to blend smoothly.
7. Spread chocolate on top of peanut butter mixture.
8. Refrigerate until cold.

Makes 24

Apple-Caramel Dessert

My neighbor MaryAnn has the reputation of being a fabulous cook. Anything she makes is mouth-watering. This dessert is no exception.

½ pound light caramels
½ cup evaporated milk

Crust:
3 cups flour
¼ cup sugar
½ cup butter
¼ cup cooking oil
1 egg, unbeaten
¼ cup cold water

Filling:
8 cups peeled and sliced apples
1 cup sugar
⅓ cup flour
2 to 4 tablespoons lemon juice

Topping:
1 8-ounce package cream cheese, softened
1 egg
⅓ cup sugar
½ cup chopped walnuts

1. Melt caramels with milk over boiling water.
2. Keep over hot water and set aside.
3. For crust, sift together flour and sugar and cut in butter until fine.
4. Add oil. Blend egg and water together into flour mixture.
5. Roll mixture out to fit a jelly roll pan.
6. For filling, combine apples, sugar, flour, and lemon juice and blend well.
7. Place in pastry-lined pan.
8. Drizzle caramel sauce over apples.
9. Beat together cream cheese, egg, and sugar until smooth. Add walnuts.
10. Spoon topping on top of apples.
11. Bake at 375° for 30 to 35 minutes.

 Serves 36

Until I come and take you away to a land like your own land, a land of corn and wine, a land of bread and vineyards.

—Isaiah 36:17

Creamy Cream Puffs

My sister Lois showed me how easy these cream puffs were to make. I particularly like them filled with French vanilla pudding

1 stick butter

1 cup boiling water

1 cup flour

¼ teaspoon salt

4 eggs

2 6-ounce servings cook-and-serve French vanilla pudding

3 cups milk

1 12-ounce container frozen whipped topping, thawed

1. Mix together butter, water, flour, and salt in medium saucepan. Cook over medium heat, stirring until mixture forms a soft ball that does not separate.
2. Remove from heat and cool slightly. Add eggs one at a time. Beat after each egg is added.
3. Beat until mixture is smooth.
4. Drop batter onto greased cookie sheet.
5. Bake at 450° for 15 minutes, then lower oven to 325° for 25 minutes.
6. Cut off tops of puffs and pull unbaked dough out and toss away.
7. In medium saucepan, mix together the pudding and the milk. Cook according to package directions.
8. Remove from heat and cool, but keep stirring. Combine with the whipped topping and fill cream puffs.

✿ Makes 12

Pistachio Dessert

Pistachio ice cream is one of my favorites. This reminds me a lot of that ice cream. I like to add chopped pistachios on top for an especially good treat.

1 stick butter or margarine

2 stacks Ritz crackers, crushed

3 tablespoons powdered sugar

2 3.4-ounce packages pistachio pudding mix

1½ cups milk

½ gallon vanilla ice cream, softened

1 8-ounce container frozen whipped topping, thawed

1. Melt butter and add crushed crackers and sugar, mixing well.
2. In a greased 9" × 13" dish, line the bottom with cracker mixture, saving some for top.
3. Beat together pudding mix and milk with electric beater for 2 minutes.
4. Add ice cream.
5. Add whipped topping.
6. Fold together and spread in pan.
7. Sprinkle crumbs on top.
8. Can be refrigerated or frozen. If frozen, soften to room temperature to serve.

✿ Serves 15 to 18

Old-Fashioned Bread Pudding Dessert

Here's another recipe for bread pudding. Five simple steps and it's ready to go. No wonder it's a favorite of many.

2 cups milk
4 cups bread crumbs
½ cup butter, melted
½ cup sugar
1 cup golden raisins
2 eggs, beaten
1 teaspoon cinnamon

1. Heat milk to scalding.
2. Put bread crumbs into 1½ quart buttered baking dish. Pour milk over bread crumbs.
3. Cool.
4. Mix rest of ingredients with bread mixture.
5. Bake at 350° for 40 to 45 minutes or until toothpick inserted comes out clean.

🍲 Serves 8

Banana Graham Cracker Icebox Dessert

My friend Doug was telling me how good his Grandmother Virginia's banana icebox dessert was, so I asked him if she would be willing to share the recipe. She did, and he's right. It's delicious.

Vegetable cooking spray
1 cup graham cracker crumbs
½ cup vegetable shortening
½ cup butter or margarine, softened
4 cups powdered sugar
2 teaspoons vanilla
2 eggs
3 large bananas
1 12-ounce container frozen whipped topping, thawed

1. Place graham cracker crumbs (reserving some for topping if desired) in 9" × 13" dish pan sprayed with vegetable cooking spray.
2. Combine the shortening and softened butter; cream together using electric mixer.
3. Beat in sugar until smooth.
4. Add vanilla and eggs. Beat well.
5. Put dollops of mixture on top of crumbs. Spread evenly with spoon.
6. Slice bananas and place on top of frosting mixture.
7. Top with whipped topping.
8. Sprinkle with graham cracker crumbs, if desired.
9. Refrigerate for 4 to 6 hours before serving.

🍲 Serves 12 to 14

Frozen Strawberry Tarts

Freeze these longer when you want to take them to a party.

1 10-ounce package strawberry halves, thawed
1 envelope Dream Whip whipped topping mix
½ cup cold milk
½ teaspoon vanilla
1 15-ounce can sweetened condensed milk
½ cup lemon juice
½ teaspoon almond extract
10 tart shells

1. Drain strawberries and reserve juice.
2. Prepare Dream Whip with milk and vanilla.
3. Mix condensed milk, lemon juice, almond extract, and strawberries with 3 tablespoons of reserved juices.
4. Blend in prepared Dream Whip.
5. Spoon in tart shells and freeze at least 4 hours.

Makes 10

Miniature Cheesecakes

Everyone loves cheesecake, and these little mini ones are like a bite of heaven. Try them for your next carry-in.

Graham cracker crumbs
2 8-ounce packages cream cheese
1 3-ounce package cream cheese
¾ cup sugar
3 large egg yolks
3 egg whites
¾ cup sour cream
2½ tablespoons sugar
1 teaspoon vanilla
Cherry halves, drained

1. Butter sides and bottoms of 4 miniature muffin tins; sprinkle with graham cracker crumbs and shake.
2. Mix together cream cheese, sugar, and egg yolks.
3. Beat egg whites until very stiff and fold into above.
4. Fill tins almost to the top.
5. Bake at 350° for 15 minutes.
6. Remove and cool. They will fall a little.
7. Mix together sour cream, sugar, and vanilla.
8. Drop mixture on the cooked cakes and bake at 400° for 5 minutes.
9. Put drained cherry halves on top.

Makes 48

Pineapple Dessert

This easy dessert was a favorite of Kathi's mom and dad. It'll become a favorite of yours as well if you like pineapple.

1 11-ounce box vanilla wafers, half of them crumbled

1 cup butter, softened

3 cups powdered sugar

4 whole eggs

2 envelopes Dream Whip whipped topping mix

1 cup crushed pineapple

1. Layer the intact cookies on bottom of a greased 9" × 13" dish.
2. Cream together butter and powdered sugar.
3. Beat in eggs one at a time.
4. Make Dream Whip according to package directions. Then fold in powdered sugar mixture and beat with electric mixer for 2 minutes. Stir in crushed pineapple.
5. Top with crumbs.
6. Refrigerate for 4 to 6 hours.

 Serves 12 to 15

Apple Dumplings

Apple dumplings are reminiscent of old-fashioned comfort cooking. Bring a little comfort to those you love by whipping up a batch of these simple dumplings.

1 8-ounce tube refrigerated crescent rolls

2 large tart apples, peeled and quartered

1 cup sugar

1 cup orange juice

½ cup butter or margarine

½ teaspoon cinnamon

1. Unroll crescent dough and separate into 8 triangles.
2. Roll up one apple wedge in each triangle.
3. Pinch edges to seal.
4. Place in greased 8" square baking dish.
5. In small pan, bring sugar, orange juice, and butter to a boil.
6. Pour over dumplings.
7. Sprinkle with cinnamon.
8. Bake uncovered at 350° for 20 to 25 minutes.
9. Serve warm with whipped cream or ice cream.

Serves 8

Excellent Chocolate Dessert

There's a reason why this recipe is named Excellent Chocolate Dessert—because it is excellent! Give it a whirl and see how you like it.

1 cup flour
1 stick margarine
½ cup pecans
1 12-ounce container frozen whipped topping, thawed
1 cup powdered sugar
1 8-ounce package cream cheese, softened
1 6-ounce package instant chocolate pudding
3 cups milk

1. For the first layer, cream together flour and margarine and add pecans.
2. Bake at 350° for 15 minutes in a greased 9" × 13" baking dish. Cool thoroughly.
3. For the second layer, mix half of whipped topping with powdered sugar and cream cheese.
4. Spread over first layer.
5. Chill for 30 minutes.
6. For third layer, mix pudding with milk and beat with electric mixer for 2 minutes. Spread on top of cream cheese mixture.
7. For final layer, spread remaining whipped topping on top.

Makes 12 to 15

Peach Crisp

I'm always asked to bring my peach crisp to carry-in events. And there is never any left over to take home. I prefer to use frozen peaches—in my opinion, they are almost as good as fresh peaches, and they let you enjoy this wonderful dessert any time of the year.

Vegetable cooking spray
½ cup sugar substitute
½ cup brown sugar
2 tablespoons cornstarch
1 teaspoon cinnamon
¼ cup low-fat margarine, melted
¼ cup water
2 16-ounce bags frozen peaches

Topping:
½ cup quick cooking oats
6 to 9 large rectangles cinnamon graham crackers, crushed
½ cup sugar substitute
1 egg white
2 tablespoons low-fat margarine, softened

1. Preheat oven to 350°.
2. Spray a 9" × 13" baking dish with vegetable cooking spray.

continued

(*Peach Crisp—continued*)

3. In a large bowl, mix together sugar substitute, brown sugar, cornstarch, cinnamon, margarine, and water.
4. Put peaches into mixture and toss with mixture.
5. Put into prepared pan.
6. In a medium bowl, combine ingredients for topping, blending them together.
7. Sprinkle over peaches.
8. Bake for 30 minutes or until bubbling and firm.

 Serves 12

*And she gave the savoury meat and
the bread, which she had prepared,
into the hand of her son Jacob.*

—*Genesis 27:17*

Peachy Dessert

This dessert will appeal to peach lovers. You may use fresh peaches in place of frozen peaches if desired.

¾ cup flour

1 3-ounce package white chocolate cook-and-serve pudding

1 teaspoon baking powder

1 egg, beaten

½ cup milk

½ cup sugar

3 tablespoons melted margarine

1 16-ounce package frozen peaches, thawed and drained

1 8-ounce package cream cheese, softened

⅓ cup half-and-half

½ teaspoon cinnamon

4 teaspoons sugar

1. In a medium bowl, stir together flour, pudding mix, and baking powder.
2. In another bowl, combine egg, milk, ½ cup sugar, and melted margarine. Add to flour mixture.
3. Spread in greased 8" square baking dish.
4. Chop peaches and place over batter.
5. Beat together cream cheese and half-and-half.
6. Pour over peaches.
7. Combine 4 teaspoons sugar and cinnamon. Scatter over peaches.
8. Bake at 350° for 40 to 50 minutes.

 Serves 9

Lemon Cheese Pie

This recipe has been a staple in Anita's family for the last twenty-five years. It's easy to make and has a great lemon flavor.

1 8-ounce package cream cheese, softened
2 cups milk
1 3-ounce package lemon instant pudding mix
1 9" prepared graham cracker crumb crust

1. Place cream cheese in a bowl and mix with electric beater.
2. Add ½ cup milk, a little at a time, blending until mixture is very smooth.
3. Add remaining 1½ cups milk and pudding mix.
4. Beat with electric mixer for about 2 minutes.
5. Pour into crust.
6. Chill until set.

 Serves 8

Madolin's Peanut Pie

Isn't everyone's favorite candy bar a Reese's Peanut Butter Cup? It sure is mine. This pie reminds me of a peanut butter cup with chocolate and peanut butter all mixed together.

1 8-ounce package cream cheese, softened
9 ounces of peanut butter, chunky or creamy
1 14-ounce can sweetened condensed milk
12 ounces frozen whipped topping, thawed
1 10" prepared graham cracker crust
4 Reese's Peanut Butter Cups chopped up

1. With electric mixer, mix together cream cheese and peanut butter until smooth.
2. Add condensed milk and half of whipped topping, reserving some for the top.
3. Mix well and pour in pie shell.
4. Top with remaining whipped topping and candy bar pieces. Put in refrigerator to chill for at least 2 hours.

Serves 8

Pauline's Strawberry Pie

Lois's long-time friend and former neighbor used to make this pie and bring it to her during the strawberry season. She knew how much Lois loved it, and I think you'll like it, too.

1 quart strawberries

1 cup sugar

¼ cup water

¼ teaspoon salt

3 tablespoons cornstarch

2 teaspoons lemon juice

Red food coloring

1 baked 8" or 9" pie shell

1 8-ounce container frozen whipped topping, thawed

1. In medium saucepan, mash 1 cup of the strawberries. Set remaining whole berries aside.
2. Add sugar, water, salt, and cornstarch to berries and mix with wire whisk.
3. Cook over medium heat until thick.
4. Remove from heat and add lemon juice and red food coloring.
5. Cool. Add remaining whole berries to mixture in saucepan and pour into pie shell.
6. Top with whipped topping.

Serves 8 to 10

Give Us S'More Pie

I was visiting Marilyn in Las Vegas when she made this pie for the first time. Since it wasn't setting up fast enough, I suggested we put it in the freezer. When we opened the freezer, the pie fell out and splattered all over us, so we had to make s'more pie.

1 12-ounce Hershey's chocolate candy bar

30 regular marshmallows

¾ cup milk

12 ounces hot fudge sauce

1 9" prepared graham cracker crust

1 8-ounce container frozen whipped topping, thawed

1. Break candy bar into pieces.
2. In saucepan, stir broken candy pieces, marshmallows, and milk until all is melted and well blended.
3. Remove from heat and cool.
4. Spread hot fudge sauce over bottom of graham cracker crust.
5. When candy mixture is cool, blend it with 1½ cups of the whipped topping
6. Pour over hot fudge sauce.
7. Spread with remaining whipped topping.
8. Refrigerate for 3 hours.

Serves 8 to 10

Sky-High Pie

Strawberries and whipping cream just go together. This is a keep-it-simple recipe that has an elegant taste.

2 egg whites

1 cup sugar

1 10-ounce package frozen strawberries, thawed slightly

1 tablespoon lemon juice

¾ cup whipping cream

1 teaspoon vanilla

1 9" prepared graham cracker crust

1. Beat egg whites with electric mixer at high speed until they peak. Add sugar gradually, beating with electric mixer, until egg whites are stiff.
2. Mix together strawberries and lemon juice.
3. Fold whipping cream into strawberry-lemon juice mixture and add vanilla.
4. Pour into graham cracker crust.
5. Refrigerate for 4 hours.

Serves 8

Delightful Pumpkin Pie

When Janene gave me this pumpkin pie recipe, I knew it had to be good. Anything with a can of frosting and whipped topping in it has to be good. She always makes this during the holiday season.

1 16-ounce can sour cream frosting

1 cup sour cream

1 cup canned pumpkin

1 teaspoon cinnamon

½ teaspoon ginger

¼ teaspoon cloves

1 8-ounce container frozen whipped topping, thawed

1 10" prepared graham cracker crust

1. Mix together all ingredients except whipped topping and crust. Beat for 2 minutes with electric mixer on medium.
2. Fold in 1 cup of whipped topping.
3. Pour into pie crust.
4. Spread remaining whipped topping over pumpkin mixture.
5. Refrigerate for 4 hours.

Serves 8 to 10

Pecan Pie

This pecan pie will warm your body and your soul. It's the ideal dessert any time of the year. This is my sister Marilyn's recipe and my favorite pecan pie.

4 eggs
1 cup sugar
1 cup light Karo syrup
½ tablespoon flour
¼ teaspoon salt
1 teaspoon vanilla
¼ cup butter, melted
½ cup pecans
1 10" prepared pie crust, unbaked

1. In medium bowl, beat eggs well.
2. Beat in sugar and syrup with whisk or electric mixer.
3. Beat in flour, salt, and vanilla.
4. Add melted butter.
5. Stir in pecans.
6. Pour mixture into pie crust and bake at 350° for 50 to 60 minutes until almost set in center.

Serves 8 to 10

German Chocolate Pie

Shirley gave me this recipe before leaving Ohio in 1987. Even if you're too full for dessert, when you feast your eyes on this, you'll want some.

⅓ cup margarine or butter
⅓ cup brown sugar
⅓ cup pecans
⅓ cup coconut
1 9" graham cracker crust
1 6-ounce serving vanilla cook-and-serve pudding
4 ounces sweet chocolate, broken up
2½ cups milk
Whipped topping
Coconut

1. Combine margarine, brown sugar, pecans, and coconut in saucepan and cook until margarine is melted.
2. Pour into pie crust.
3. Combine pudding, chocolate, and milk in saucepan and cook until mixture boils.
4. Remove from heat; if needed, beat to blend.
5. Cool for 5 minutes.
6. Pour into pie shell.
7. Chill for 4 hours.
8. Spread with whipped topping and garnish with coconut.

Serves 8

Lemon Pie

Lois's luscious lemon pie combines sweetness and tartness in just the right amounts. If you don't want to make the meringue for the top, use whipped topping.

1 4-serving package lemon pie filling, not instant
²⁄₃ cup sugar
¼ cup water
3 egg yolks
2 cups water
2 tablespoons lemon juice
2 tablespoons butter
1 9" pie crust, baked
3 egg whites
6 tablespoons sugar

1. Combine filling, sugar, and ¼ cup water in saucepan.
2. Mix in egg yolks.
3. Add 2 cups water.
4. Cook and stir to a full boil, about 5 minutes.
5. Cool 5 minutes.
6. Blend in lemon juice and butter.
7. Pour into cooled baked pie crust.
8. Beat egg whites until foamy.
9. Gradually beat in sugar, beating to stiff peaks.
10. Spread over the filling.
11. Bake at 425° for 5 to 10 minutes or until lightly browned.

 Serves 8

Coconut Cream Pie

When I take this to a friend, I usually add toasted coconut flakes to the top of the whipped topping. It gives it a nice garnish and flavor.

2 3-ounce packages French vanilla instant pudding
3 cups cold milk
1 12-ounce container frozen whipped topping, thawed
1 teaspoon coconut flavoring
1 cup flaked coconut
1 9" prepared graham cracker crust

1. In large bowl, combine pudding with milk.
2. Beat with an electric mixer for 3 minutes.
3. Fold in half of the whipped topping.
4. Add flavoring and coconut.
5. Pour into crust.
6. Spread remaining topping over pudding mixture.
7. Refrigerate for 3 to 4 hours.

Serves 8 to 10

Picture Perfect Peach Pie

This recipe from my collection had been written down by my brother-in-law Jim many years ago. Since I love peaches, it's become a real favorite of mine.

1 3-ounce package peach gelatin
²/₃ cup boiling water
1 cup French vanilla ice cream
1 cup sliced fresh peaches or frozen peaches, thawed (plus extra for garnish, if desired)
1 8-ounce container frozen whipped topping, thawed
1 9" graham cracker crust

1. Dissolve gelatin in boiling water.
2. Add ice cream; stir with whisk until smooth.
3. Blend in fruit and whipped topping.
4. Spoon into crust.
5. Chill 3 to 4 hours.
6. Garnish with fresh peaches.

Serves 8

Split Pie

This banana split pie has all the toppings of a banana split minus the hot fudge. Make this on a moment's notice, and you'll be sure to please your family and friends.

1 10" graham cracker crust
2 8-ounce packages cream cheese, softened
2 cups confectioners' sugar
2 sliced bananas
1 2-ounce can crushed pineapple, drained
½ cup sliced fresh strawberries
1 12-ounce container frozen whipped topping, thawed

1. Mix cream cheese and confectioners' sugar and spread on crust.
2. Put sliced bananas over cream cheese.
3. Spread can of drained crushed pineapple on top.
4. Add fresh strawberries.
5. Top with whipped topping.

Serves 8 to 10

Vegetables

Giving Is Receiving

So many of these recipes that I've included in this cookbook are quick and easy to prepare but still full of flavor. Food is an integral part of our daily lives in so many ways. It's been that way since the beginning of time.

We celebrate with food, and we mourn with food. Whenever we have joyful events such as birthdays, weddings, anniversaries, church socials, office parties, and picnics, food takes on a major role. Conversely, whenever a family or friend loses a loved one, we then turn to food as well. One of the first things we do is prepare dinner to help comfort, console, and show our concern. We always put a little of ourselves into our cooking and add at least a cup of love.

The gift of food is always appropriate. You may need to make it sugar-free for your diabetic friend, low-calorie for those watching their weight, or otherwise tailor it to a special need. The act of giving is an outward sign that says, I care about you, I am here for you.

At potluck suppers and church events, everyone usually brings a dish they know others will enjoy. These are wonderful sources for good recipes. When we give to others, it always seems that we receive more than we give. I know how much I have appreciated the kindness and thoughtfulness of others for sharing these recipes and how much they warmed my heart. Don't wait for a special occasion or a time of need to take someone a dessert or casserole. Make someone's day—it will make your day a good one, too!

Broccoli Rice Casserole

In our "hurry and wait" world of today, recipes that are as easy as this one are welcomed by most cooks. Short on time? You can also buy celery and onion already chopped in small containers or packages in your grocer's produce department.

Cooking spray

4 tablespoons butter

½ cup chopped celery

½ cup chopped onion

1 10.75-ounce can cream of mushroom soup

1 soup can of milk

1 cup mushroom stems and pieces

½ cup sliced water chestnuts

1 10-ounce package frozen chopped broccoli, thawed and drained

2 cups cooked rice

Salt and pepper to taste

1 8-ounce jar Cheese Whiz

½ cup bread crumbs

1. Coat 9" × 13" baking dish with cooking spray.
2. Melt butter in skillet and sauté celery and onions for 2 or 3 minutes over medium heat.
3. Stir in the soup and milk, blending with a whisk. Heat until warm.
4. Remove from heat and add mushrooms, water chestnuts, broccoli, rice, salt, and pepper.
5. Put the mixture in the prepared 9" × 13" baking dish.
6. Cover with the Cheese Whiz.
7. Top with bread crumbs.
8. Bake at 350° for 30 to 45 minutes.

Serves 12 to 15

Ye shall eat nothing leavened; in all your habitations shall ye eat unleavened bread.

—Exodus 12:20

Calico Baked Beans

Remember how long it used to take your mom to make homemade baked beans? These "homemade" beans have an extra added appeal—sausage. You can use the hotter version if you want to really spice things up.

1 16-ounce package sausage

1 15.25-ounce can lima beans

1 15-ounce can kidney beans

1 28-ounce can baked beans

1 5-ounce can tomato sauce

½ cup chopped onion

½ cup brown sugar

1. Brown sausage in skillet until cooked and drain well.
2. Mix all ingredients together in large bowl.
3. Put in greased 9" × 13" baking dish and bake at 350° for one hour.

Serves 8 to 10

Copper Pennies

My friend Nanette's mom gave her this recipe, and it's one of Nanette's favorites. I wasn't sure about it when I read the ingredients. But now that I've tried it, I can recommend it highly.

2 pounds carrots, thickly sliced

1 10.75-ounce can tomato soup

½ cup oil

1 cup sugar

1 tablespoon Worcestershire sauce

1 teaspoon dry mustard

1 onion, sliced in rings

1 green pepper, sliced in strips

1. Cook carrots in saucepan just covered with water until tender. Drain.
2. In medium bowl, mix all remaining ingredients. Add carrots to bowl. Cover and marinate overnight.
3. Bake at 350° for 30 to 45 minutes.
4. Can be served warm or cold.

Serves 10

Tater Tot Casserole

I love the addition of smoked sausage to this casserole. I double the sausage for the "big" meat eaters when we go to summer picnics.

2 16-ounce cans green beans, drained
1 10.75-ounce can cream of mushroom soup
1 10.75-ounce can cream of celery soup
1 cup diced onions
16 ounces smoked sausage
1 16-ounce bag frozen tater tots, thawed

1. Mix green beans, soups, and onions in bowl.
2. Place mixture in greased 9" × 13" baking dish.
3. Dice smoked sausage into small pieces and place on top of green bean mixture.
4. Top with tater tots.
5. Bake at 350° for 1 hour.

 Serves 8 to 10

Zucchini with Stuffing

Everyone who has a summer garden seems to have an overabundance of zucchini and they're nice enough to share with those of us who don't have gardens. I chop the zucchini extra-fine so some of my finicky eaters don't know it's in this recipe.

6 cups chopped zucchini
¼ cup chopped onions
1 6-ounce box stovetop dressing
½ cup margarine, melted
½ cup shredded carrots
1 10.75-ounce can cream of chicken soup
1 cup sour cream

1. Put zucchini and onions in saucepan just covered with ¼ cup water and bring to boil. Simmer for 3 minutes. Drain well.
2. Combine stovetop dressing with ½ cup melted margarine.
3. Layer half of dressing mix on bottom of greased 9" × 13" baking dish.
4. Mix zucchini and onions with carrots, soup, and sour cream.
5. Put zucchini layer on top of dressing.
6. Top with the remainder of dressing.
7. Bake at 350° for 25 minutes.

Serves 8 to 10

Cauliflower Casserole

Cauliflower is one of my favorite vegetables, cooked or raw. You can substitute cream of mushroom soup or cream of chicken soup in this recipe for a little variation.

1 medium head cauliflower, broken into florets
1 cup sour cream
4 ounces shredded Cheddar cheese
1 10.75-ounce can cream of celery soup
½ cup crushed cracker crumbs
½ cup Parmesan cheese
Paprika

1. Place cauliflower and a small amount of water in a saucepan.
2. Cover and cook for 5 minutes or until crisp-tender.
3. Drain.
4. Combine cauliflower, sour cream, cheese, soup, and crumbs and put into greased 8" × 8" square baking dish.
5. Sprinkle with Parmesan cheese and paprika.
6. Bake at 325° for 30 minutes.

Serves 6

Pepper's Beans

Pepper's beans are an essential ingredient for any picnic. What's a picnic without hot dogs, hamburgers, and baked beans? Take these to your next picnic.

¼ cup chopped green pepper
½ stick butter
2½ cups northern beans, cooked
1 14.5-ounce can diced tomatoes, drained
1 medium onion, thinly sliced
½ teaspoon dry mustard
½ cup sugar
1 tablespoon vinegar
½ teaspoon salt

1. Sauté green pepper in butter in large skillet.
2. Add remaining ingredients.
3. Put into a greased 9" × 13" baking dish.
4. Bake at 350° for 45 to 60 minutes.

Serves 8 to 10

Easy Homemade Mac 'n' Cheese

I haven't made homemade macaroni and cheese in years. When I received this recipe, I gave it a whirl. I have to say I did like it better than the packaged ones I've been using.

1 16-ounce box of elbow macaroni

½ stick butter

2 eggs

1 8-ounce package shredded Colby cheese

1 cup milk

1. Boil macaroni until done. Drain.
2. Add butter, milk, and eggs to macaroni. Mix well.
3. Add half package of cheese. Stir until cheese melts.
4. Pour into 8" square baking dish and put rest of cheese on top.
5. Bake at 400° until cheese is melted and slightly brown.

ॐ Serves 6

Crispy Broccoli Casserole

Laura has been generous and kind to share so many of her "scrump dillyumptious" recipes with me for this book. This recipe is great as it is, but since I'm such a cauliflower lover, I like to use 1½ pounds broccoli and 1½ pounds cauliflower.

Vegetable cooking spray

3 pounds frozen broccoli florets, thawed

4 eggs, slightly beaten

2 cups cottage cheese

2 tablespoons minced onion

2 teaspoons Worcestershire sauce

3 cups shredded Cheddar cheese

¼ cup butter, melted

2 cups bread crumbs

1. Spray 9" × 13" baking dish with vegetable cooking spray.
2. Drain broccoli and pat dry with paper towel.
3. In large bowl, mix together eggs, cottage cheese, onion, Worcestershire sauce, and Cheddar cheese.
4. Line baking dish with broccoli. Pour cheese mixture over broccoli.
5. Add bread crumbs to melted butter and stir with fork.
6. Spoon this over top of casserole and pat down. Cover broccoli flowers so they are not exposed to the heat.
7. Bake at 350° for 30 minutes.

ॐ Serves 8 to 10

Laura's Cauliflower Gratin

For those of you who don't have a food processor, try substituting regular bread crumbs. Since cauliflower is one of my favorite vegetables, I intend to use this recipe often. Thanks again, Laura, for sharing.

Bread Crumb Topping:

4 slices sandwich bread with crust, cut into quarters

2 tablespoons unsalted butter, softened

¼ teaspoon salt

⅛ teaspoon ground black pepper

Filling:

4 quarts water

1 tablespoon salt

3 pounds cauliflower florets

2 tablespoons unsalted butter

2 tablespoons minced shallots

1 minced garlic clove

1 tablespoon flour

½ cup heavy cream

Pinch nutmeg

Pinch cayenne

Salt

⅛ teaspoon ground black pepper

½ cup and 2 tablespoons grated Parmesan cheese

1 teaspoon fresh thyme leaves, minced

1. In a food processor, pulse bread, butter, salt, and pepper in 10 1-second pulses until the mixture resembles coarse crumbs. Set aside.
2. Heat oven to 450°.
3. Boil 4 quarts of water and add 1 tablespoon of salt and the cauliflower.
4. Cook 3 to 4 minutes until outsides are tender but inside is crunchy.
5. Drain cauliflower, rinse in cold water, and drain again.
6. Heat butter in a large skillet about 2 minutes. Add shallots and garlic and cook about 30 seconds until fragrant.
7. Stir in flour until combined.
8. Whisk in cream and bring to boil.
9. Stir in nutmeg, cayenne, ¼ teaspoon salt, pepper, ½ cup Parmesan, and thyme until it is blended.
10. Turn off heat and combine cauliflower with sauce.
11. Transfer mixture to greased 2-quart baking or gratin dish.
12. Sprinkle the remaining 2 tablespoons of cheese over the top.
13. Sprinkle the bread crumb topping over the top.
14. Bake 10 to 12 minutes at 350° until golden brown and the sauce bubbles around the edges.

Serves 6 to 8

Mashed Sweet Potatoes

I love this recipe from Shirlee, another Beavercreek Friend of the Library volunteer. I've grown tired of all the super-sweet sweet potato recipes with marshmallows and lots of brown sugar. What a pleasant change this is. Of course, I still use extra butter when serving.

2 15-ounce cans yams, drained
4 tablespoons butter
½ cup hot cream
2 tablespoons dry sherry or bourbon
1 cup dry bread crumbs
½ teaspoon paprika
2 teaspoons butter

1. Place yams in a large mixing bowl and begin mashing.
2. Add 4 tablespoons butter, cream, and sherry.
3. When fully mashed, remove yams from bowl and place in a greased 8" square casserole.
4. Mix together bread crumbs, paprika, and 2 teaspoons butter and spread on top of potato mixture.
5. Bake at 350° until crumbs are brown.

❧ Serves 8

Spinach Soufflé

I don't have many recipes for spinach casseroles—just one, actually. The Tabasco sauce gives this dish a bit of a bite, but it's quite good.

2 10-ounce packages frozen chopped spinach
½ cup butter
¾ cup cracker crumbs
¼ cup grated onion
2 eggs, beaten separately
⅛ teaspoon dried thyme
1 teaspoon garlic powder
3 dashes Tabasco sauce
½ teaspoon pepper
¼ cup Parmesan cheese
½ teaspoon salt

1. Preheat oven to 350°.
2. Cook spinach according to directions on the package.
3. Drain well and combine with the remaining ingredients.
4. Pour into greased 2-quart casserole.
5. Bake at 350° for 30 minutes.

❧ Serves 6 to 8

Sweet and Spicy Beans

My dear friend Linda just recently e-mailed this bean salad to me. I really liked the addition of corn to this recipe. In fact, you could use a can of Mexican-style corn in place of the regular corn.

1 15.5-ounce can red kidney beans, rinsed and drained

1 15.25-ounce can whole kernel corn, rinsed and drained

1 15-ounce can black beans, rinsed and drained

1 15-ounce can black-eyed peas, rinsed and drained

1 2-ounce jar diced pimientos, drained

4 green onions, sliced, approximately ½ cup

⅓ cup sugar

⅓ cup red wine vinegar

⅓ cup salad oil

½ teaspoon ground red pepper

½ teaspoon salt

1. In a large bowl, combine kidney beans, corn, black beans, black-eyed peas, pimientos, and green onions.
2. Whisk together sugar, red wine vinegar, oil, red pepper, and salt.
3. Pour vinegar mixture over bean mixture and toss to coat.
4. Cover.
5. Chill for at least 2 hours or up to 24 hours.
6. Serve with a slotted spoon.

Serves 8 to 10

Traditional Black Beans and Rice

When Laura's daughter-in-law comes to visit, she prepares this dish for her, as she is a vegetarian. I was glad to get this recipe as I am always looking for vegetarian recipes for my son, who also eats no meat.

1 tablespoon olive oil

¾ cup finely chopped onion

½ cup finely chopped green pepper

1 cup diced tomatoes

1 15-ounce can black beans, drained and with juice reserved

½ teaspoon thyme

1 teaspoon garlic salt

3 tablespoons cider vinegar

½ teaspoon hot pepper sauce

2 cups cooked rice

1. In a large skillet, heat olive oil.
2. Cook onion and green pepper until tender.
3. Stir in tomatoes, beans, thyme, and garlic salt.
4. Cook 3 minutes.
5. Add vinegar, pepper sauce, and reserved juice.
6. Continue to cook for 5 minutes.
7. Serve over rice.

Serves 6 to 8

Spinach Pie

Sharon, my dear friend from Virginia, sent me this. She relayed that this makes two pies and that you'll need both of them when you're making these for "take-out." The smoked pork chops add a perfect taste to the spinach and cheese.

3 tablespoons oil
2 large onions, chopped
2 10-ounce packages frozen spinach, thawed and dried
4 or 5 smoked pork chops, trimmed and diced
1½ cups grated Parmesan cheese
1 cup ricotta cheese
4 eggs, slightly beaten
2 deep dish pie crusts

1. Preheat oven to 425°.
2. Sauté onion and spinach in oil for 2 minutes.
3. Add remaining ingredients and pour into unbaked pie shells.
4. Bake 35 minutes or until done.
5. Cool 10 minutes and cut into serving wedges. Can cut into smaller wedges for appetizers.

⠘ Serves 12 to 16

Vegetable Quiche

I am always glad that my sister-in-law Gayle brings this veggie quiche for our family gatherings. Since I am interested in serving vegetarian dishes, this one is very welcome.

Vegetable cooking spray
1 16-ounce package frozen broccoli, thawed or cooked
⅓ cup chopped onion
¼ cup chopped green pepper
1 cup shredded cheese
1½ cups milk
¾ cup Bisquick
3 eggs

1. Spray 9" pie pan with vegetable cooking spray.
2. Mix broccoli, onion, green pepper, and cheese in pie plate.
3. Beat remaining ingredients until smooth.
4. Pour over vegetable mixture.
5. Bake at 375° for 45 to 60 minutes until golden brown.

⠘ Serves 6 to 8

Spinach Rings

This recipe only makes 6 to 8 servings, so when making this for a party, you might want to double the recipe. These would also be good with a white cream sauce.

Vegetable cooking spray
½ cup chopped onion
1 egg
½ teaspoon salt
⅛ teaspoon black pepper
1 10-ounce package frozen spinach, thawed and drained
8 strips of bacon, uncooked

1. Sauté onion in pan sprayed with vegetable cooking spray.
2. In mixing bowl, beat together egg, salt, and pepper.
3. Add spinach and onions. Mix well.
4. Grease bottoms of standard muffin tins and line sides with bacon. Cut to fit.
5. Place spinach mixture in lined tins.
6. Bake at 350° for 15 to 20 minutes.
7. Remove from tins and serve.

Makes 6 to 8

Baked Ziti

When Sally asked me if I would like to have a meatless entrée recipe, I responded with a resounding "Sure would." When my vegetarian son, Tim, comes to visit, I'll be sure to fix it for him. He loves pasta—I know he'll like this.

1 16-ounce package ziti, cooked
2 cups cottage cheese
1 32-ounce jar spaghetti sauce
1 teaspoon oregano
1 teaspoon garlic powder
½ teaspoon onion powder
8 ounces shredded mozzarella cheese

1. Mix all ingredients except mozzarella.
2. Spread in a greased 9" × 13" baking dish.
3. Sprinkle with mozzarella cheese.
4. Bake at 350° for 30 to 45 minutes.

Serves 8 to 10

Wild Rice Amandine

Wild rice has such a nutty flavor—I just love it. You could substitute brown rice for the white rice that Judee uses in this recipe. I would double this when taking out.

¼ cup white rice

¾ cup wild rice

¼ cup margarine

2 tablespoons chopped onion

2 tablespoons dried chives

2 tablespoons finely chopped green pepper

2½ cups chicken broth

¼ cup finely chopped almonds

1. Mix white rice with wild rice; wash and drain.
2. In heavy saucepan, heat margarine and stir in chopped onions, chives, and rice.
3. Cook over gentle heat, stirring until rice begins to turn yellow.
4. Remove from heat and add green pepper.
5. Stir in chicken broth and add almonds.
6. Put into greased 8" square baking dish and cover.
7. Bake at 300° for 1 hour and 15 minutes.

 Serves 6 to 8

Barb's Best-Ever Potato Salad

Cousin Barbara tells me this is the *only* potato salad she will ever make any more. It's become her favorite recipe. Although she prefers the Italian dressing, she uses whichever one she has in the fridge.

7 medium potatoes, cooked in jacket, peeled, and sliced

⅓ cup clear French or Italian dressing

¾ cup sliced celery

⅓ cup sliced green onions, including tops

4 chopped hard-cooked eggs

1 cup mayonnaise

½ cup sour cream

1½ teaspoons prepared horseradish

1 teaspoon mustard

1. In medium bowl, pour dressing over hot, cut-up potatoes.
2. Marinate several hours or overnight in refrigerator.
3. When ready to serve, add celery, green onions, and eggs to potatoes.
4. In small bowl, combine mayonnaise, sour cream, horseradish, and mustard and stir together.
5. Pour over salad and toss well.

Serves 8 to 10

Fruity Sweet Potatoes

My cousin Barbara's mother-in-law, Dorothea, shared this recipe with her. I love the pairing of apricots and sweet potatoes along with the buttery apricot sauce. This is fantastic!

2 23-ounce cans yams, drained

1 23.5-ounce can of apricots, drained and with liquid reserved

1¼ cups brown sugar

1½ teaspoons cornstarch

1 teaspoon grated orange rind

⅛ teaspoon cinnamon

1 cup apricot juice from can of apricots

2 tablespoons butter

½ cup pecan

1. Mix yams and apricots in greased 9" × 13" baking dish.
2. In saucepan, mix brown sugar, cornstarch, orange rind, cinnamon, and apricot juice.
3. Bring to a boil, stirring constantly until thickened.
4. Add butter and pecans.
5. Pour over potatoes and apricots.
6. Bake at 375° for 25 minutes.

Serves 8 to 10

Gemuse

This is an old Siegfried family favorite handed down by my Grandma Siegfried, who came from France with her husband and children in 1911. We all pronounce it *guh-meese*, which is the German word for "vegetables." You can use any vegetables; just mash them separately and mix them in with your prepared mashed potatoes. As the song goes, "Memories are made of this"!

5 pounds potatoes

½ pound carrots

3 stalks celery, chopped

4 onions, peeled and diced

1½ sticks butter

½ cup milk

1 cup sour cream

1. Peel potatoes and cut into bite-size pieces. Cover with water in 5-quart pan.
2. Add carrots, celery, and onions.
3. Cook over medium heat until vegetables are tender.
4. Drain vegetables, separating carrots.
5. Mash carrots in separate bowl.
6. In large bowl, mash potatoes, celery, and onions by hand.
7. Add butter and milk and beat with electric mixer.
8. Beat in sour cream.
9. Put into greased 9" × 13" baking dish.
10. Top with ½ stick of butter and keep warm at 250°.

Serves 8 to 10

Asparagus and Pasta

This is one of only a few casserole recipes I have using asparagus. Asparagus is not quite as economical to use as other frozen vegetables. So if you're making this casserole and want to cut costs a little, try frozen broccoli or spinach.

8 ounces uncooked spaghetti, broken into thirds

2 tablespoons margarine

3 tablespoons flour

2 cups milk

1 cup shredded mozzarella cheese

Dash pepper

1 16-ounce package frozen asparagus spears, thawed

1 13.25-ounce can sliced mushrooms, drained

2 tablespoons Parmesan cheese

1. Cook spaghetti to desired doneness. Drain. Keep warm.
2. Preheat oven to 400°.
3. Grease 9" pie pan.
4. Melt margarine in medium saucepan and stir in flour until smooth and bubbly.
5. Gradually add milk with wire whisk. Blend well.
6. Cook over medium heat 6 to 10 minutes, stirring constantly, until mixture thickens.
7. Add mozzarella and pepper.
8. Spoon spaghetti into greased pie pan.
9. Top with asparagus, then mushrooms.
10. Pour white sauce on top.
11. Sprinkle with 2 tablespoons Parmesan cheese.
12. Bake 20 minutes or until mixture is bubbly.

🍴 Serves 6 to 8

And ye shall serve the LORD your God, and he shall bless thy bread, and thy water; and I will take sickness away from the midst of thee.

—Exodus 23:25

Menu Ideas

New Year's Day

Bob's Won Tons, 12
Reuben Roll-Ups, 49
Pork Tenderloin and Potato Bake, 79
Spinach Salad with Mushroom
    Dressing, 112
Anything Goes Cake, 155

Memorial Day

Georgia's Fried Chicken, 57
Tater Tot Casserole, 200
Calico Baked Beans, 199
Applesauce Salad, 110
Banana Graham Cracker Icebox
    Dessert, 184

Veteran's Day

Mom's Mashed Potato Soup, 128
Open-Faced Stroganoff Loaf, 41
Veggie Salad, 108
Lois's Yummy Salad, 113
Turtle Cake, 146

Easter

Stuffed Ham Rolls, 80
Fruity Sweet Potatoes, 209
My Favorite Seven-Layer Salad, 102
Sweet Potato Biscuits, 25
Old-Fashioned Bread Pudding
    Dessert, 184

Father's Day

Shrimp Cocktail Appetizer, 5
Braised Chuck Rosemary, 45
Gemuse, 209
7-Up Salad, 110
Cheese Biscuits, 30
Summer Lemon Cake, 143

Christmas

Cranberry Chicken Salad, 116
Spinach Salad, 109
Fruit Salad, 181
Poppy Seed Bread, 28
Angel Squares, 176

Mother's Day Brunch

My Sisters' Favorite Coffeecake, 16
Cinnamon Crunch Muffins, 20
Chicken Quiche, 54
Strawberry Salad, 105
Creamy Cream Puffs, 183

July Fourth

Five-Hour Barbecue, 43
Cole Slaw, 113
Barb's Best Ever Potato Salad, 208
Macaroni Salad, 102
Apple Dumplings, 186

And having food and raiment let us be therewith content.

—*I Timothy 6:8*

Index